Like Jennifer, I have learned through children what Jesus can do. He has chosen the simple, humble, and childlike to reveal His power and love to the world. This book is rich encouragement for all who are hungry to receive impartation from "the least of these." The children and youth of today are riding a rising wave of revival that should enrich us all with ever-increasing signs and wonders. Let them teach you about the kingdom!

—HEIDI BAKER, PhD
FOUNDER AND DIRECTOR, IRIS GLOBAL

In every generation a cry arises from the very heart of God. Jennifer Toledo is one of those voices who echo the cry of God's heart! Having raised my own four kids in the supernatural culture, I know what Jennifer teaches in the pages of this book works! I know it is effective. And I know that you can create a culture for the supernatural for your kids too! Empower the children to do the works of Jesus! An army is waiting to be awakened and released!

—JAMES W. GOLL
FOUNDER OF ENCOUNTERS NETWORK AND AUTHOR OF *ANGELIC ENCOUNTERS*, *THE SEER*, AND *A RADICAL FAITH*

Few things challenge and inspire me like the stories of what God is doing and has done. In *Children and the Supernatural* Jennifer Toledo does an incredible job of challenging the church to take a second look at how we view children by telling their stories. I even found my own perspective being challenged. But I also found the stories of these children, their faith, and their encounters with God stirred my heart to believe for more in my own life and to press in deeper with Jesus. I should not have been surprised. Every time I encounter the ministry of Jennifer, my heart is alive with faith and I am provoked to my core to believe God for greater things. Without question this book will not only challenge your perspective of children but also call you to believe for more of God in your own life.

—BANNING LIEBSCHER
DIRECTOR, JESUS CULTURE

A child growing up in the world today has no chance unless they know the real Jesus—not the Jesus of religion. This book will make a difference in your child's future!

—SID ROTH
HOST, *IT'S SUPERNATURAL!*

I'm in love with *Children and the Supernatural*. I seriously cried the whole time I read it. This is not just a book; it is a piece of God's heart that will reach inside of you and transform the way you think. Although, like many people, I had an awareness of the subject, I was wrecked with responsibility to see children empowered and set free to lead. Jennifer Toledo's work sets a foundation that you may never have fully imagined regarding the global calling on the next generation. This is not a book just for children's workers; it is an epic story and foundational tool for valuing half of the world's population, who happen to be young. I have never been so inspired by children. I was given so much hope for what God is doing and wants to do with children when I read this book. This isn't just inspiration. This book should be required reading for any Christian. It gives a glimpse into the supernatural power of God at work in the earth today and imparts transferable faith.

—SHAWN BOLZ
SENIOR PASTOR OF EXPRESSION58, STUDIO CITY, CALIFORNIA
AUTHOR OF *KEYS TO HEAVEN'S ECONOMY*, *THE THRONE ROOM COMPANY*, AND *THE NONRELIGIOUS GUIDE TO DATING*

Children and the Supernatural will absolutely touch you to the core, provoke you, build your faith, and cause you to both laugh and cry! The younger generation needs to know God, and they need to know His power. Through Jennifer Toledo's book you will be refreshed as you discover God's heart for children today. Jennifer not only writes on this subject, but she also lives it!

—PATRICIA KING
FOUNDER OF XPMEDIA, XPMINISTRIES, AND XPMISSIONS
MARICOPA, ARIZONA

Jennifer Toledo is a champion of children. Her personal commission from God to give children the "authentic gospel" has revolutionized her life and the lives of all the children she teaches. Children in her ministry have seen AIDS patients healed and demons cast out, and they have experienced the presence of God in overwhelming ways. Jennifer is an outstanding example and teacher. As those who have been advocates for at-risk children for years, we know the underdeveloped potential of children throughout the globe, so it is with joy that we highly commend both Jennifer and this book!

—WESLEY AND STACEY CAMPBELL
FOUNDING PASTORS, NEW LIFE CHURCH
KELOWNA, BRITISH COLUMBIA, CANADA

Children

and the

Supernatural

JENNIFER TOLEDO

CHARISMA
HOUSE

Most Charisma House Book Group products are available at special quantity discounts for bulk purchase for sales promotions, premiums, fund-raising, and educational needs. For details, write Charisma House Book Group, 600 Rinehart Road, Lake Mary, Florida 32746, or telephone (407) 333-0600.

Children and the Supernatural by Jennifer Toledo
Published by Charisma House
Charisma Media/Charisma House Book Group
600 Rinehart Road
Lake Mary, Florida 32746
www.charismahouse.com

Unless otherwise noted, all Scripture quotations are from the New International Version. Copyright © 1973, 1978, 1984, International Bible Society. Used by permission.

Scripture quotations marked GW are from GOD'S WORD translation of the Bible. Copyright © 1995 by God's Word to the Nations. Used by permission of Baker Publishing Group.

Scripture quotations marked KJV are from the King James Version of the Bible.

Scripture quotations marked NKJV are from the New King James Version of the Bible. Copyright © 1979, 1980, 1982 by Thomas Nelson, Inc., publishers. Used by permission.

Scripture quotations marked THE MESSAGE are from *The Message: The Bible in Contemporary English*, copyright © 1993, 1994, 1995, 1996, 2000, 2001, 2002. Used by permission of NavPress Publishing Group.

Visit the author's website at www.gcmovement.org and www.expression58.org.

Library of Congress Cataloging-in-Publication Data:
Toledo, Jennifer.
  Children and the supernatural / Jennifer Toledo. -- 1st ed.
      p. cm.
  Includes bibliographical references (p.   ).
  ISBN 978-1-61638-606-1 (trade paper) -- ISBN 978-1-61638-717-4 (e-book)
1. Children--Religious life. 2. Supernatural. I. Title.
  BV4571.3.T65 2012
  248.2083--dc23
                                        2012010340

12 13 14 15 16 — 987654321
Printed in the United States of America

I WOULD LIKE TO DEDICATE THIS BOOK to my own amazing beautiful children, Malaika, Josiah, and Ruah, who are a constant reminder in my life of the beauty and power of being childlike. You each carry such a special piece of God's heart, and I am absolutely in love with you! Thank you for being so patient with me as I wrote this book. I pray that you each have a lifetime of incredible experiences with our supernatural Father and that you will always be rooted in His love.

I WOULD ALSO LIKE TO DEDICATE THIS BOOK to the countless men and women who have faithfully, year after year, sown into the lives of children. You are true unsung heroes. Many of you have served when no one else would, believed for things no one else dared to, and took on a ministry that for years has lacked proper honor in the body of Christ. Thank you. Your faith and love have not been in vain.

CONTENTS

Acknowledgments xi

Foreword by Bill Johnson xiii

Introduction................................xv

Part One: The Back Story

  1 **The Children of Bungoma**.....................1

Part Two: Encountered

  2 **Designed for Encounter**......................29

  3 **A Radical Invitation**..........................37

  4 **A Butterfly, a Breakthrough, and Angels**.....41

  5 **A Date With Jesus**...........................53

  6 **When God Shows Up** 69

  7 **Conner's Encounter**..........................79

Part Three: Prayers That Change History

  8 **Prayers That Shift Laws**......................89

  9 **One Million Angels** 93

 10 **When Prayers Shake Darkness** 99

Part Four: Releasing Children to a Broken World

 11 **Finding Barb** 105

 12 **The Children of Colima** 109

 13 **Saved By Smiley Faces** 115

 14 **Orange and Banana**.........................119

 15 **"God Loves You and Your Tattoos!"**.........123

 16 **The Perfect Treasure Hunt** 127

 17 **The Shoe Shiner**...........................131

Part Five: Healing Hands

 18 **Malaria Healed** 135

 19 **When a Baby Releases Healing** 137

ix

20 Healings in Everyday Places 141

21 The Body Parts Room in Heaven 143

22 The Newt. 147

23 Esther—the Miracle Worker 155

Part Six: A Child Shall Lead Them: The Role of Children in Global Revival

24 The Divine Setup 159

25 From Slave to Royalty 163

26 Who Are the Masses? 169

27 Generational Unity—the Key to Global Revival . . .177

28 A Tree and a Chainsaw .185

29 A Recurring Dream 189

30 The 4/14 Window—the Golden Age of
    Opportunity. 191

    Notes 197

ACKNOWLEDGMENTS

SOMEONE ONCE TOLD me that I should write a book because hardly any women in the their twenties and thirties were writing books and those voices needed to be heard. Although I couldn't agree more with this person's comment, I now understand why women my age aren't writing books—it's because trying to write a book while having babies is like trying to juggle flaming torches blindfolded. (Trying to write a complete thought with a toddler climbing all over you, a mountain of laundry staring you down, and Barney blaring in the background is no easy feat!)

So many people helped to bring this book to life:

- First of all, Jona—my amazing husband who constantly cheered me on, took three kids to the park a thousand times, and lovingly made me coffee every time I asked (which was a lot). You are a gift and the absolute love of my life.

- My dear friend and Kenyan brother Patrick Siabuta, who lived several of these stories with me and spent countless hours tracking people down for me.

- All of my friends and family who encouraged me to write out these precious stories and to not care whether people believed they were true.

- The incredible fathers and mothers in my life who have believed in me, celebrated me, and encouraged me in this process. Thank you for your endorsements and for your constant support.

- My publishing company (particularly Maureen Eha) for pursuing me and pulling this book out of me.

- All the awesome children who shared their special stories with me (and the awesome parents who allowed me to tell them).

- And most importantly—this book would not exist without these stories, and these stories would not exist without the incredible and powerful love of God interacting with mankind. God is very much alive and very much still on His throne. For that, I am wholeheartedly grateful!

I hope you enjoy the book.

FOREWORD

Jennifer Toledo has written an amazing book that just couldn't be more timely. It is a record of her experiences in seeing the kingdom of God manifested through the hearts, hands, mouths, and lives of children. Her awareness of their gifts and capabilities brings a necessary wake-up call to us as we recognize the need to equip this generation to "do the stuff." The stories in this book are provoking as we read about the childlike faith that empties hospitals, brings salvation to the person on the street, and is quick to obey and trust the voice of God.

The world is crying out for a credible witness to the resurrection of Jesus Christ—faith that is intensely authentic and effective. And just as God caught the attention of the world through a child in a manger two thousand years ago, so now He speaks of His purposes and plans through children in a way that even adults can understand.

God sees differently than we do. As a result, He constantly uses children as a standard from which grown-ups are measured. We must become like children to receive the kingdom fully. Many years ago my dear friend Dick Joyce told us over and over again, "Children don't get a junior Holy Ghost!" I have lived with that conviction and priority ever since. But Jennifer has taken this idea to a level that demands attention.

I can no longer just agree with the concept. I must adjust my life to illustrate this priority of heaven. This book is not only contagious; it is also dangerous—dangerous to both the political spirits and the religious spirits that want to keep the power of childlikeness away from the front burner of the church. For if we participate in a breakthrough of that nature, nothing will be impossible for us.

Children and the Supernatural is a simple yet profound record of God's view of people. Yes, it has fabulous stories about children being used by God in powerful ways. That in itself is mind-boggling. But it's more than that. This book reveals the child's heart that is so attractive to God, and it tells why. Whether you are a parent, a person involved in children's ministry, or just a grown-up who is tired of being so grown up that you miss the kingdom, this book is for you. It's an invitation to see as God sees and value what God values. This is a personal charge to go higher by going lower. Get ready to be amazed.

I want to see this book in the hands of every parent I pastor and everyone who works with children. But equal in importance to me is to see this book read by adults who don't have children but have a hunger for the lifestyle of Jesus. I long to see people read this book to discover how to become like the child God favors so much in Scripture. This book has potential to stir and instill hunger in everyone who reads it. It is that provoking. Simplicity in devotion to Christ, practicality in focus and ministry, all come forth from *Children and the Supernatural*.

—BILL JOHNSON
PASTOR, BETHEL CHURCH, REDDING, CA
AUTHOR, *WHEN HEAVEN INVADES EARTH* AND *ESSENTIAL GUIDE TO HEALING*

INTRODUCTION

WILL YOU TEACH the next generation the undiluted gospel?" I heard the Lord speak those words while I was sitting in the dirt with a couple of street children in Kenya, and they forever changed the course of my life. My first response was, "Lord, I was raised in America. I'm not sure I know the undiluted gospel." I was overwhelmed by the desperation and desire I heard in His voice. His words felt like electricity in my body.

There have been only a few times in my life when I've heard the Lord so clearly. I sat there completely undone as waves of emotion swept over me. I was so instantly aware of the deep longing in His heart for a generation to know Him as He truly is. There was a desperation and passion so present in His voice. He wanted to be known on His terms, without religiosity, without unbelief, without cultural mindsets, without politics. Just known. I couldn't hold back my tears, "Lord, if You will teach me the undiluted gospel, I will teach the next generation."

That was one of those pivotal moments in my life, a crossroads where my perspective and priorities forever shifted. I was twenty-one years old. I had been in the church my whole life, and yet I suddenly felt I needed to relearn everything. I began to reevaluate what I believed about God, asking Him to teach me from His perspective. I felt so challenged and provoked all at the same time. Sometimes God's perspective offended me. Other times I realized how many things I said or did were actually rooted in the Christian culture around me rather than the authentic culture of Christ's kingdom. I felt like a child again, and it was so liberating.

During this time I was living in western Kenya in a town called Bungoma. I was working with an amazing group of people who loved children, and I was contributing to the work however I could. I spent most of my afternoons meeting with a small group of kids, most of whom were orphans or living on the streets, and I began to share with these precious children everything God was teaching me. I often found myself stumbling through a teaching, trying to find language to communicate truth without attaching my natural, human perspective to it.

The children were like sponges, and the fruit of truth quickly became apparent in their lives. It was so much fun to watch them come alive. I had a few dear friends in Kenya, most of whom were local ministers who shared my passion for kids and were pouring into the city's children as well. The caretakers of the homes where some of the children stayed told me stories of how sometimes at night they would wake up to the sound of a room full of children worshiping and interceding because they had been so gripped by the truth of who God is.

Many children in Bungoma began to receive deep revelation during their encounters with God. They were freed of addictions, fears, and hopelessness, and they became so vibrant in their relationship with God that it started to spill out onto others. God in His love had brought me to Bungoma, a town that was already beginning to be stirred, a place where children were destined for greatness. He brought me to Bungoma to relearn the gospel—through the eyes of a child.

I'll tell you the full story of what happened with the children in Bungoma in just a moment. But before I do, you need to know that one encounter I had sitting in the dirt, hearing the desperation of the Father longing for a generation to truly know Him, changed me. I became keenly aware of heaven's pursuit of this generation and God's unyielding passion to capture their hearts.

I've spent a lot of time thinking about and observing how we do church. Oftentimes we adults send the kids off to go be entertained so we can have "real" church. We send them off to watch videos, play games, and eat their little snacks so we can explore the deep things of God. I began to feel so saddened by this and could understand to some extent how the Father's heart must grieve over this. The reality is, if you have been born again, you are part of the body of Christ with full access to everything in the kingdom. Age doesn't matter. God is passionate about encountering children, and for so long children have been held back from the deep things of God.

Jesus's words ring loud and clear: "Let the little children come to me, and do not hinder them, for the kingdom of heaven belongs to such as these" (Matt. 19:14).

God longs to bring children into the fullness of who He is. That is where they've always belonged. All over the earth God is revealing Himself to the young. I am continually amazed and thoroughly delighted to occasionally peek in to this beautiful exchange. Children are such great receptors because they simply believe God. They don't have unbelief, disappointments, and theology standing in the way. They are wide-open vessels, and God is filling them.

May we all become students of the undiluted gospel. It's not just about the young encountering God. It's about a whole generation of people on the earth being awakened to the reality of who He is! God is revealing Himself to the young and old alike so we can see Him with the right lenses. He is good, He is faithful, He is fun, He is kind, He is powerful, He is involved, and He is so in love with us! May we all become students of the undiluted gospel. My prayer is that the stories that follow will provoke and inspire you to childlike faith once again.

PART ONE

THE BACK STORY

Let the little children come to me, and do not hinder them, for the kingdom of God belongs to such as these.

—Mark 10:14

THE CHILDREN OF BUNGOMA

OR YEARS I have wrested with even telling the stories of the children of Bungoma because they are holy and precious to me, and I feared they wouldn't be believed or that some angry, unbelieving person somewhere would try to quench the beauty of what took place. I have since come to realize that there is nothing and no one who can ever detract from what we witnessed and the amazing fruit that has come out of God encountering these children. The world needs to hear of His great works, and I'll leave God to defend Himself.

God did something so amazing in and through the children of Bungoma that it left me forever changed. On my first trip to Kenya in 2001 I was surprised by the general lack of value given to children. Children were to be seen and not heard. Child abuse rates were high. Children could be seen living alone on the streets with no one to take care of them. Free education didn't exist, so masses of children weren't going to school. And, sadly, children were virtually invisible in most of the churches I visited.

Pastors commonly "shooed" the kids away to make space for the adults. When asked how many people attended their church, the pastors rarely even counted the children. Most shocking of all, many people believed children should not even be allowed to get saved until they were adults, a belief

1

I later discovered was common in many other places in the world.

When I arrived in Bungoma, I realized that mind-set was also prevalent in this relatively small community in western Kenya near the Uganda border. I fell in love with the children of Bungoma, and my heart ached for them to be restored to their rightful place of value. The good news is that the justice of heaven isn't like taking a negative number and elevating it to zero. The justice of heaven is like taking a negative number and adding to it until it is more than a thousand!

That is exactly what God did. He put Himself on display through the children of Bungoma. I was in good company, as I was living with a dynamic couple, Pastors Patrick and Mary Siabuta, who were just as passionate about the children as I was. Patrick was instrumental in starting a citywide network of children's pastors (Bungoma Pastors Fellowship Children's Department), which would become the backbone of what God was about to do. Patrick had been sharing the message that God could use children with the other leaders, and things began to shift in the city.

After I heard the Lord ask me if I would teach the next generation the undiluted gospel, I began to meet with a small group of about thirty children. As I mentioned earlier, most of the children were orphans or street kids, and the Lord began to encounter them in a deep and profound way. The children would weep as they encountered His love and His presence. They would be set free from an "orphan" spirit and begin to understand who they were as sons and daughters of God. Children who had been living on the streets addicted to sniffing glue were delivered from their addictions and fell in love with Jesus. Within no time these kids were so full of Jesus that it was apparent we needed to help create some outlets for them to share what God was putting in their hearts.

WHEN A CHILD'S HEART SINGS

Patrick and I arranged for a group of twelve children to go to the local government hospital, which is called the District Hospital. It's the largest hospital in the region and is full of sickness, sadness, and death. It was very overwhelming at first. Not only were our senses on overload because of the smells, the scenes, the sounds, the pain, the suffering, and so on, but the patients didn't seem excited to see us. There were forty to seventy people per room, and patients were suffering from malaria, typhoid fever, AIDS, and more.

The environment was so intense that the children began to shrink back, overwhelmed by the situation. I pulled the children aside and lovingly reminded them that we didn't have to "do" anything in our own strength. We simply needed to listen for the Father's instructions and do whatever He said to do. That seemed to put them a little more at ease, and we just waited on heaven's instructions. We were in the first ward at the time, and one of the boys, Richard, came up to me and nervously said, "Auntie, I think I'm supposed to sing a song." Now, time out. You need to hear Richard's story to truly appreciate this moment.

Richard comes from the Turkana people, a remote, indigenous group in northern Kenya. The Turkana are nomadic shepherds who live much like they've lived for thousands of years. The Turkana region was hit severely by horrific drought and famine, and Richard's family had struggled to survive. Because of the extreme hardships, Richard and his twin sister were given away to elderly relatives shortly after their birth. Richard's parents went on to have two more children, and when Richard was only five years old, his mother, who was pregnant again, was beaten to death by his father.

His father fled the village and is said to have been killed in response to his actions. It was a horrible tragedy, and Richard grew up much as other Turkana orphans do. He was passed from one person to the next until, finally, he was able to walk and could be given a few animals to "tend." He survived as a very young boy in the blazing desert by suckling from the roaming camels and goats. He was alone and unprotected; that is, until a man who called Himself "Jesus" began to visit him in the desert.

This man would talk to young Richard, telling him that one day He would rescue him out of this place and that He would always love him and care for him. In mid-2000, when Richard was just seven years old, my friend Patrick and his bishop came to know Richard's village, Kachoda, while distributing food up in the drought-stricken desert in the north. The two ministers learned that there were seven orphans in the village who desperately needed care. A few months later, in early 2001, a team of people including Patrick and two dear friends of mine, Ralph Bromley and Noel Alexander, made the long trek out to find them and bring them back to their children's home in Bungoma, Kenya.

When the village leaders heard of these strange white men who wanted to take their children, they became nervous and told the children these foreigners would probably eat them and they should not go with them. Although Richard didn't understand much of what these white men were saying, he heard them say they knew Jesus. So he confidently went with them and told the others, "They may eat me, but they say they know Jesus, and they are going to send me to school— and I believe them and that is all that matters." That is how sweet Richard came to live in Bungoma at the children's home I was working with at the time. Due to the resistance, only four of the seven orphans came along. Richard met Jesus as his Lord and Savior and always walked around with a beaming smile and a heart of gratitude.

That sunny day as we took our first steps in the hospital, Richard felt the Lord leading him to sing a song. I had no idea what might happen, but I encouraged Richard to do whatever the Lord was putting on his heart. He nervously moved in front of the group. Everyone in the room looked at him with irritation. But Richard just closed his eyes and focused all of his love and affection on the man Jesus, who had rescued him out of the desert. Richard began to sing the old hymn "I Surrender All" with the most tenderness and love you've ever heard. This little boy lifted his hands to heaven, tears streaming down his face, and he just began to worship with abandon. It was truly one of the most beautiful things I have ever witnessed.

I closed my eyes and was unable to restrain my tears. As Richard sang with such love, heaven came into that hospital. The atmosphere in the room dramatically shifted. The presence of God was so strong I was afraid to open my eyes. The weight of heaven was so present it felt hard to breathe. The beautiful, cracking, off-key, passionate worship of a child had unlocked a realm that overwhelmed me. I knew I was not alone. When I finally was able to open my eyes, I saw that the whole room was undone by this sudden "presence" that had overtaken us all. We didn't have to preach the gospel that day. We didn't have to convince anyone to give his life to Jesus. People began to cry out to the living God as this holy presence began to fill the room.

The children quickly dispersed and went from bed to bed, praying with people who desperately wanted to give their lives to this true and living God. Evangelism was never easier—everyone wanted this Jesus! It was such a beautiful and powerful experience for us. One little child's obedience and love made space for the King of glory to have His glory. And that was just the beginning!

A SPIRITUAL SIEGE

After the trip to the hospital the children continued to grow in the Lord, and soon other children throughout the city caught word that God could use them as well. We started hearing stories about groups of children who were gathering together to fast and pray and seek God. Patrick and I started taking every opportunity to train children's workers, Sunday school teachers, and the children themselves. It was apparent that God was stirring something in the children, and we wanted to partner with Him in it.

As the children began to encounter the Lord, many of them were getting gripped by God's heart for their city. Bungoma was a great place, but the spirit of division was deeply embedded in the churches. There were two pastoral networks in the area, and there was a lot of bitterness and division between the two groups—so much so that they had filed lawsuits and had taken their dispute to the national courts.

The children began to pray for a move of God in their city and for strategy to see healing come to their churches. During this season of prayer one little boy had a dream. In his dream he saw a large dragon in the city center. The dragon had swallowed up many people from the city. In the dream the Lord invited all the children to march throughout the city for seven days. The little boy saw that each day they marched, the dragon got weaker and weaker. Then on the seventh day the dragon could no longer survive, and it vomited up the people of the city and died. Wow! That's a pretty clear dream! The little boy shared his dream with the others, and we knew this was God's strategy! After much prayer the children really felt like we were to do a seven-day march through the city declaring life and that the city belonged to Jesus.

We began to organize and make plans for this spiritual "siege" of the city. At first some of the leaders didn't quite understand what we were doing and struggled to take it seriously. Thankfully the network of children's pastors fueled the vision, and within a short period of time we had overwhelming support from pastors, bishops, and the community. The planning committee consisted of 288 people (48 adults and 240 children). It was apparent the Spirit of God was with these children and that they weren't just "playing" church. They were a real force to be reckoned with.

We called for children all over the city who loved Jesus to join us for seven days of taking the city back for Jesus. The children decided that they wanted to do more than march; they wanted to go throughout the city in teams—to the hospitals, the police station, the marketplaces, the schools, and so on—and release the kingdom of God. So we organized morning outreaches that would be followed by afternoon marches. They then decided that we most certainly should finish the day with open-air crusades in the middle of town (fully run by children). That seemed like a perfectly amazing idea to me. I was so excited I could hardly wait. At this point I had returned to the States to gather a team of children and youth to bring with me back to Kenya. We arrived in August 2002, and you could sense the excitement in the air. The atmosphere was ripe after months of prayer and expectation.

The morning before everything was to begin we organized a large breakfast for all the pastors of the city and the children from each of their churches. We gathered at the Bungoma Tourist Hotel with 150 children and various pastors, parents, and key city officials. The top police chief was present, as well as Mr. Kisingu, the head of the District Prison. The children wanted the blessing of their fathers and wanted to honor them as they stepped out into what they felt the Lord calling them to do. I believe this step of honor was hugely pivotal in the spirit, and something definitely happened that morning.

Although I don't know whether all the pastors present truly were carrying vision for the children or genuinely believed they would be used significantly, they certainly were kind enough to extend their blessing. After months of sharing the vision and advocating for what God could do through children, many of the city's pastors had rallied behind the children and were contributing however they could. These pastors, as a prophetic action, handed a large wooden key to the children, releasing them to take the spiritual keys of the city and inviting them to do whatever God had placed in their hearts. What a beautiful moment that was!

That evening all the children returned to their churches to gear up for the next day. I was walking in town and decided to stop by a church called Deliverance Church, which was very involved in the siege. Because of its prime location, many of the children had gathered there for trainings and prayer times. In fact, this church was the prayer-training center for all the children from twelve different churches.

Many of the children had been participating in a week-long fast and had gathered at this church to pray and worship. I could hear the children as I passed by and decided to go in. I sat in the back of the church, loving every moment as I watched the children dance and worship in full force on the platform. All of a sudden something crazy took place. A large poisonous snake fell from the rafters above right onto the pulpit near where the children were dancing.

Everyone screamed and jumped (including myself— eww!), and a wonderful brave man sitting up front leaped up, smashed it, and threw it outside. When my heart finally stopped racing, it became clear to us that this was a picture. The snake represented the "strongman" of disunity falling as the children were blessed and released to take their place in the city and as generational unity was unleashed.

I believe it was significant that the snake fell as the children were leading worship. The generational unity that the city entered into that morning made way for revival in the land! Amazingly enough one of the little girls who was present that day previously had a dream in which she saw a snake fall from the sky and break into pieces on the ground. She shared the dream with the other children and her leaders and declared prophetically that the snake of the city would fall. We celebrated and danced all the more. We knew victory was ours, that God was with us—and the strongman of division had fallen!

BUNGOMA CHILDREN FOR JESUS

The next morning we launched our seven-day siege. We weren't sure how many children would show up to participate, but we knew the kids who were coming were passionate lovers of Jesus and full of faith! The kids were glowing. Many of them were wearing matching shirts, and they carried the most amazing little homemade signs with slogans such as "Bungoma Children for Jesus" or "Jesus Is Lord." My heart was overflowing with pride in these gorgeous children. I could feel the absolute joy and pleasure of the Father over them and their faith!

We started the mornings off by sending teams of children all over the city. One day we went into schools. The children shared the love of Jesus with other children, ministering hope and life, and they led many other kids to Jesus. They went to the police headquarters and ministered to the officers and their families. Many police officers were saved and healed, and they encountered love and freedom through the ministry of the children. They blessed businesses and ministered to shopkeepers. They even went door-to-door just loving on anyone they could find.

One morning we sent out 124 children to lead street evangelism. We gave them some basic instructions, prayed over them, and anointed them for the task. Many carried decision certificates, and we assigned various adults to intercede and provide security for the children. The response was phenomenal! In one of the groups three children (two girls and one boy) approached a group of women who were selling vegetables. The children ministered the gospel to these women with such passion, boldness, and assurance; it was remarkable to see.

Then the children asked if any of the women would like to receive Christ as their Savior. They were visibly moved, and one woman immediately fell down onto her knees and started to cry aloud. The children were startled because they never expected her to cry. Suddenly a man approached, trying to sort out what was going on. The kids got scared and thought maybe they had done something wrong. But one of the adult leaders came up and explained to the gathering crowd that this woman was crying in repentance of her sins.

The crowd continued to watch as the children led the woman in a prayer of salvation, and afterward three more people from the crowd joined in and wanted to get saved as well. It was a very special moment on the street that day, and the fruit that was harvested was incredible. In just a few hours that morning we recorded that more than 250 people made a decision for Christ and nineteen healings took place on the street.

In addition to this, we sent a team of children to every single hospital and health center in town, and the stories of healing are astounding! Here is a glimpse of what happened in the hospitals that week.

As our team of children accompanied by a few adults

entered one particular hospital, several of the children had an open vision in which they saw what looked like a "demonic animal" sitting on one of the hospital beds. They were shaken by what they saw and immediately began to pray. One of the children felt like God was showing them that "a stronghold of death" was in the place, and the animal represented that stronghold. After a time of prayer the children were growing concerned because the creature was not leaving. Our team began to ask the Father what they should do, and one of the kids said, "It's not leaving because it has the right to be here, but God said if we worship, it will go."

That's exactly what they did. The children began to sing and worship and fill that hospital room with praise. Within moments, all at the same time, the children saw the animal turn into an "Indian woman" and run out the door. The children chased her out the door, and she "disappeared" once outside. The children danced and cheered and then began to pray for the patients in the hospital. So many healings took place that day—the atmosphere was wide open for healing!

The most amazing part is that after this stronghold of death was taken out, there was a dramatic reduction in deaths at that hospital. We were able to track the number of deaths at that hospital for one whole year after this. People were amazed at the significant difference and knew God had done something special. Death is usually a daily occurrence in hospitals in third world countries, so this truly was a sign and a wonder! This wasn't the only miracle that took place at this hospital. When we first visited, the entire compound was run-down, dirty, and had unsafe working conditions. The nurses feared the cracks in one of the wards would cause part of the building to collapse on them. After the children visited and prayed and the spiritual atmosphere shifted, there was also a dramatic shift in the natural environment. Shortly afterward the government authorized an entire renovation of the hospital, and to this day it is clean, safe, and entirely updated. The spiritual shift led the way for the natural shift in that place.

We were thrilled with the way God was moving in this hospital, and yet this was just one of the places the children visited. I personally helped lead the group of children who went to the large government-run hospital, Bungoma District Hospital. This hospital is the largest, most populated hospital in the region. After our first experience in the hospital with Richard and the team, my expectations were through the roof. I was confident that God was going to do amazing things that day. We divided ourselves up among the six wards. One ward was for women, one was for men, one had children, one prisoners, and so on. But there was one ward that will forever be etched into my memory. This ward was for all of the worst cases—it basically was the death ward. There were beautiful people in their last stages of AIDS and other horrible diseases. The room was full of terminally ill patients who hadn't been given much hope. In fact, it wasn't too uncommon to find a dead body still lying in the room that had not been taken out yet.

That was the case the day we went in with the children. The children were as overwhelmed as I was, but we were so full of faith and expectation. We had a beautiful time loving on and speaking life over each patient. We were able to lead many to the Lord, and we were very well received in each of the wards. Although we saw some people get saved and some testify that they were feeling "a little better," I was very dissatisfied. I was expecting crazy miracles and wanted way more than just "a little better"!

As we were leaving the hospital one beautiful little girl with huge brown eyes who was walking hand in hand with me looked up at me and said, "Wasn't that amazing?" My heart was heavy, and I was really battling disappointment, so her question caught me off guard. Trying to hide my inner argument with God, I smiled and said, "Yes, tell me what was so amazing about that?" She looked up with her eyes bright and her face filled with wonder and said, "By tomorrow all those people are going to be healed!" It was one of the moments when the reality of how pathetic and faithless I was became apparent.

I wanted faith like this child. My eyes filled with tears. I smiled at her and said, "You know what, sweetheart, you're right! By tomorrow all those people are going to be healed." I was instantly reminded of the verse in Mark 16:17 that says, "And these signs shall *follow* them that believe" (KJV, emphasis added). I could deal with that. Signs can come after I leave anytime. I settled in my spirit to be at peace about it and let God do whatever He wanted to do.

We continued with our day's activities, and first thing the next morning Patrick, my dear pastor-friend, received a call from one of the senior hospital staff asking him to come down to the hospital immediately. A few people from our team headed to the hospital to meet with the hospital staff member, and with absolute seriousness the man asked, "Who is this God you pray to?" He was shocked and overwhelmed, and with hardly any explanation he began to lead some of our team through each of the wards.

Words cannot express the beauty and joy in those rooms—they were empty! Of all six wards, only two had a few people left in them. The rest were empty! God had healed them! So many children were suffering with malaria and typhoid—they were totally healed. AIDS patients were suddenly waking in the night feeling perfectly fine. They just got up out of their beds and announced that they were healed and going home.

Some of the doctors and nurses were absolutely overwhelmed and amazed! They knew these things were not medically possible. Something supernatural had taken place. Many of them just wept showing the empty beds and telling the stories. There was story after story of how the patients just suddenly felt fine and packed up their things and left. Shocking! Mind-blowing! Beautiful! Jesus is so amazing! The head nurse of the whole region was there that day and was so moved by what God did that she went on to train other nurses in how to release "true healing" to patients when they are admitted. That precious woman to this day is still on our board of directors in Kenya and continues to carry the vision of children moving in the supernatural.

There was one particular patient who moved me greatly. She was in her last stages of AIDS and was dying. We were able to lead her to the Lord and left her with a Bible. I asked about her when we returned the next day, and she was one of the patients who suddenly announced in the night that she was totally fine. She rose up off her deathbed, packed her bag, and went home. We were able to track her down and found out that within a week she was back in the university and was completely well—giving all the glory to God!

My pastor-friend Patrick returned to the hospital a week later for a follow-up visit. It was early morning, and he and some other members of his team were in Ward Two talking with one of the nurses who had been on night duty. She said the morturary attendant had come in asking if there were any "customers." The nurse looked around and told the man there weren't any customers and that she didn't expect any soon because there were no signs any would be coming. The nurse then explained to Patrick that the "customers" the man was asking about were the dead. She said that for three days the mortuary attendant had been going around through the wards looking for the dead but had not found any. A miracle had happened, and now the man was beginning to worry about losing his job. Patrick later learned that some mortuary attendants refer to the dead as customers because their jobs depend on the death rate at the hospital.

This is our God! Our God is alive, He is powerful, He is loving, and He is good! That senior hospital staff member was undone and overwhelmed by this kind of God. We didn't have to convince people to get saved—their hearts couldn't resist Him!

After seeing so many miracles in the hospitals, the children continued to visit the hospitals and release healing even after the siege ended. The children had been visiting the largest private hospital in town for several weeks when we received a call from the head matron. The matron, who happened to be a Christian, said, "Thank you for continuing to send over the kids! So many people continue to get healed every day!"

She informed us that a group of the children, in fact, had been coming every day during their lunch break from school, and God was moving powerfully! We were thrilled at the news. Then, half-jokingly, she told us. "Well, it's wonderful what God is doing, but if this keeps happening, you'll have to pray for us all to find new jobs!"

Well, sure enough, the children continued to visit the hospital every day on their lunch break for the next couple of months. Amazingly enough, people were getting healed all the time—and usually before a doctor had even seen them.

I'll never forget the day I received a message from Patrick that the hospital matron called. She wanted us to be the first to know that so many people were being healed through the ministry of the children that the hospital had taken a huge hit financially and was going to close down. Healing had become so commonplace the hospital was no longer needed! Though sad about losing her job, the hospital matron was overjoyed to see the power of God at work through the children!

As children continued to contend for lasting fruit in their city, there was one other health center they continued to visit and pray over regularly. This particular health center was known as a place where school-aged girls and women went to obtain abortions. The children prayed fervently for the place to close down, and sure enough, within two months the facility had closed down and later became a restaurant!

RELEASING GOD'S HEART FOR THE NATION

Well, back to the story of the seven-day siege. The morning outreaches were just the beginning. Quite the kickoff, right? After each morning outreach the children would gather in various locations throughout the city to begin their daily march through the city. All the children would converge in the city center and walk the main streets of town together. What a sight this was. More than three thousand children showed up to march the streets and declare their city belonged to Jesus! They waved their flags, carried their signs, sang, danced, prophesied, and made declarations of life over Bungoma. Three thousand glorious voices in unison sang over and over again, "Bungoma children for Jesus. Hallelujah!"

We had a truck moving ahead of the masses with a large bullhorn on the back. As the children would hear the Lord share a promise over the city, they would climb up on the truck and prophesy out over the bullhorn, and all the other children would come into agreement with them. I have some of the best video footage of these marches—masses of children full of love and faith storming the streets. All "normal" business had to stop. Cars could not pass. People just lined the streets and took it all in. The children were shifting the spiritual climate of the city, and people could feel it. It was so powerful and significant—and all of this came from a strategic dream the Lord had given a little child and from the radical faith and obedience of the children to obey.

Every evening after the march the children would converge at the large soccer field in the middle of town, where we had set up a large stage and sound system for the open-air crusade. Each day the children sang out their praises, danced in joy, preached like nobody's business, and led people from the city into salvation, healing, and deliverance. The crowd gathered around, and God moved powerfully in our midst. Toward the end of the week the adults working with us were noticeably tired, but it seemed the children's strength grew each day. We were amazed at how the children seemed to get stronger, wiser, bolder, louder, and more powerful in their preaching, and how they seemed to have increased authority. They blew away everyone's expectation!

We made a rule that no child would be allowed behind the pulpit unless his or her pastors were present in the meeting. A particular group of children who genuinely felt they had a word from the Lord were disappointed because their bishop had not been attending. They decided to go to his home and camp out, demanding him to come with them to the crusade. That particular group of children showed up late for the crusade, but they came glowing and confident as their bishop was marching alongside them, singing and chanting, "Halleluiah! Hosanna! Bungoma children for Jesus!"

After seeing the children being used so powerfully, many pastors began to request that we send a team of children to their churches to minister. To this day many of the children who ministered during this siege are still very powerful ministers of the gospel! One of the most impacting moments for me was seeing a handful of pastors weeping at the altar, repenting before the Lord for not valuing these children before. The presence of God was so strong, and it was evident that children didn't need to grow up before they could be used mightily. God was setting a precedent in the city: the kingdom of God was coming to Bungoma, and it was coming through these children.

Many of the pastors began to repent for their division and judgment toward one another as they saw children from all the churches in town working and serving together. The children knew no divide, and they were modeling what could be done in a spirit of unity. The pastors were so moved by this that shortly afterward they held a public meeting where they repented of their division and washed one another's feet! This was historic for Bungoma!

After seven days of this the city was transformed! There was clearly a shift in the spiritual atmosphere. This was the beginning of transformation in the region. Over the next several months and years children throughout the region were trained in the "undiluted gospel." Thousands of children were empowered to encounter God and become voices of change for their communities. When Bungoma finally hit the map, it was known for its unity and being a voice for children. Several other communities longed for what Bungoma had experienced. Bungoma children became an inspiration to so many.

This seven-day event took place back in 2002. Since that time the fruit of what those children sowed in the spirit continues to grow. Twice since then, top government officials and leaders from all spheres of society have filled the largest venue in Bungoma (a soccer stadium) to hear the word of the Lord and the strategies for the nation God was giving to the children. The event has been broadcast on national television. National leaders have come to the children seeking out their wisdom and perspective because it's apparent that they carry the wisdom of heaven. My husband and I had the privilege of being present in the first event like this. To our amazement a caravan of senior Muslim officials showed up to hear the children. We were shocked! One of the pastors asked, "Why have you come? You know these children are Christians." The top leader answered, "What these children are doing goes beyond religion. They are changing society, so we must support them."

Wow! If that is not a testimony to the power of God, I don't know what is! The children released God's heart for the nation on issues of justice and morality, and the nation listened. They advocated for children at risk and shared the hope and strategies God had given them. It was such a monumental moment to watch. This was Bungoma—the small town that seemed to have no value for children just a short time before. The justice of heaven had come and restored children to an incredible place of honor and value within the community and the nation.

A true spirit of generational unity had been birthed, and, hand in hand, Bungoma children broke something open spiritually for children everywhere. God is not looking for someone who has it all together and knows all the answers. God is looking for friends. God is not looking for someone great and powerful. God is looking for someone with childlike faith. And He will always find them. He will always find a friend. He will always find someone with childlike faith— as long as there are children on the earth.

Bungoma was the place where God awakened me to the possibilities of what He could do with children. Bungoma was the place where I realized I needed to go on a journey of discovering the undiluted gospel. Bungoma changed me, and it was just the beginning. I had experienced something there that I knew God wanted to do everywhere. I was left deeply impacted by the power of blessing and generational unity—and I knew it was the key to break through into the deeper things of God. I became so keenly aware that if the body of Christ is ever going to demonstrate the undiluted gospel to the world, the fathers and sons have to learn to walk together.

Patrick Siabuta was one of the first pastors in Bungoma to get a vision for what God could do through children, and he began training them to pray for the sick and reach their city for Jesus.

The children of Bungoma prayed with such faith and expectation that God would move in their city.

Before the seven-day siege several pastors handed a large wooden key to the children as a prophetic act, releasing them to take the spiritual keys of the city.

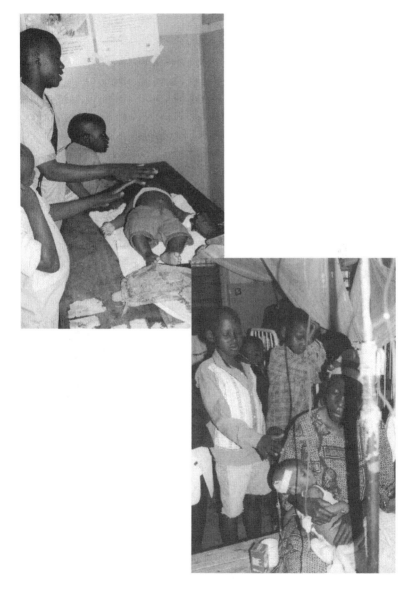

We saw incredible miracles occur when the children in Bungoma went into hospitals and prayed for the sick.

PART TWO
ENCOUNTERED

That which was from the beginning, which we have heard, which we have seen with our eyes, which we have looked at and our hands have touched—this we proclaim concerning the Word of life. The life appeared; we have seen it and testify to it, and we proclaim to you the eternal life, which was with the Father and has appeared to us. We proclaim to you what we have seen and heard, so that you also may have fellowship with us. And our fellowship is with the Father and with his Son, Jesus Christ. We write this to make our joy complete.

—1 John 1:1–4

DESIGNED FOR ENCOUNTER

T HERE IS NO greater joy than to see a child encounter the reality and the beauty of the living God. God is not distant. He is not hidden. It is His great pleasure and delight to reveal Himself to mankind. He is so passionate about connecting with us—having real relationship, real friendship, real conversation—and He will continually pursue us and draw us into that connection because it is the very reason we exist. James 4:8 says, "Draw near to God and He will draw near to you" (NKJV). I don't know about you, but this scripture always amazes me! God throws out this amazing invitation for mankind. If we will draw near to Him, He will come near to us! He longs to be seen, known, and encountered.

Children are primed for encountering God. Their purity and simplicity open them up to a realm that through the years many of us have learned to tune out. When I was pregnant with my first child, I read all the pregnancy books. I was shocked to find out that research has proved babies in the womb dream. That was mind-blowing to me. A baby living in a completely dark environment, who has never had any experiences, dreams. What do babies dream about? They've never even seen anything. They've never experienced anything. Or have they?

O LORD, you have searched me and you know me.
You know when I sit and when I rise; you perceive my
thoughts from afar. You discern my going out and my
lying down; you are familiar with all my ways. Before a
word is on my tongue you know it completely, O LORD.
You hem me in—behind and before; you have laid your
hand upon me. Such knowledge is too wonderful for
me, too lofty for me to attain.

Where can I go from your Spirit? Where can I flee
from your presence? If I go up to the heavens, you are
there; if I make my bed in the depths, you are there. If I
rise on the wings of the dawn, if I settle on the far side of
the sea, even there your hand will guide me, your right
hand will hold me fast. If I say, "Surely the darkness will
hide me and the light become night around me," even
the darkness will not be dark to you; the night will shine
like the day, for darkness is as light to you.

For you created my inmost being; you knit me
together in my mother's womb. I praise you because
I am fearfully and wonderfully made; your works
are wonderful, I know that full well. My frame was
not hidden from you when I was made in the secret
place. When I was woven together in the depths of
the earth, your eyes saw my unformed body. All the
days ordained for me were written in your book before
one of them came to be. How precious to me are your
thoughts, O God! How vast is the sum of them! Were
I to count them, they would outnumber the grains of
sand. When I awake, I am still with you.

—PSALM 139:1–18

There are so many things about this passage that I love.
First of all, God is so in tune with us! He knows absolutely
every little detail about each of us—and He has known each

of these unique things before we were ever born. Not only does He fully know us, but this passage also demonstrates that God longs to be near us.

- "You hem me in—behind and before" (v. 5).

- "You have laid your hand upon me" (v. 5).

- "Where can I go from your Spirit? Where can I flee from your presence?...Even there your hand will guide me, your right hand will hold me fast" (vv. 7, 10).

God's presence, His Spirit is inescapable! God is passionate about being near us. God wants us to encounter Him. That is why Jesus went to the cross—so mankind would never have to be separated from God's love and His presence. Heaven is motivated by a desire to love and connect with humanity. In verses 13–16 we see how present, how near, how involved God is with each person while he or she is still in the womb. He personally weaves together each intricate part of who we are in the secret place.

Not only that, but God also writes a story for each one of us before we're ever born. He dreams up a beautiful story for our life while shaping us in the quiet dark of the womb. That is amazing! I tell people all the time, "Boredom is a choice." If you're bored in your life, that is not God's fault. God— the ultimate Creator, the King of creativity—has dreamed up an amazing, adventurous love journey for you, and He wrote this amazing story for you while you were still in your mother's womb.

We being the powerful, free creatures we are have the

power to choose our destiny. We can go through life holding the steering wheel and becoming a product of our circumstances and choices. Or we can learn to walk in union with God and live out the beautiful dream He has for our lives. I guarantee you that the ultimate Creator did not write a boring, powerless, depressing story for you!

One of my favorite parts of Psalm 139 is in verses 17 and 18:

> How precious to me are your thoughts, O God! How vast is the sum of them! Were I to count them, they would outnumber the grains of sand. When I awake, I am still with you.

God's thoughts toward us are overwhelming! They are unending. And God has these thoughts while we are still in the womb. God is so very present. We are the object of His love and affection. He surrounds us. He wraps us in His presence, and He breathes life into us—all while we are still in the womb. Babies are nurtured and soaked in the presence of God while in the womb. All they know is spirit. Their bodies are still being formed, but their spirits are surrounded in the presence of God. That is amazing!

So what do babies dream about? Dreaming is one way the brain processes information. Babies in the womb have mass amounts of information to process as they are interacting with the presence of God and being formed in His life and goodness. They're taking it all in and learning to "process" spiritual activity.

I love the end of verse 18—"when I awake, I am still with you." Whether "awake" is intended to mean awake from sleeping or "when I am born," the promise remains. God is saying, "I am still with you." We are with Him, and nothing changes.

Once we're born, heaven's pursuit of us never changes. His thoughts toward us don't change. His desire to be near us doesn't change. His presence surrounding us doesn't change. And His wild love story for our lives doesn't change.

What if, from their birth, we taught our children how to continue to live out of their spirits? What if we nurtured their spiritual sensitivity and equipped them to never lose their discernment? What if we refused to belittle what they saw and experienced by calling it "imagination" and instead raised them to think seeing and experiencing things in the spirit was "normal"? As Matthew 5:8 says, "Blessed are the pure in heart, for they will see God."

MALAIKA, WHAT DO YOU SEE?

When my first child was born, I was always intrigued to see her eyes dart across the room as she stared with fascination at some invisible thing. This happened quite a lot. I'll never forget a time when she was about fourteen months old and was sitting on my lap one evening in our living room. All of a sudden her eyes started darting back and forth across the room. With great fascination on her face she pointed up toward the ceiling and became very still, hardly moving for almost fifteen minutes. (Now, parents, you know when a fourteen-month-old is still for that long, something supernatural must be going on!) She would look around and smile, and then her eyes would grow bigger. She seemed very serious.

I sat there in amazement and could feel the presence of God in the room. After a while I whispered to her, "Malaika, what do you see? What is God doing? Can you show Mama what the angels are doing?" I did not expect my fourteen-month-old to really comprehend the request, but I genuinely hoped she would. Malaika quickly turned around to me, with a very serious look on her face, her eyes still following something I couldn't see. She extended one of her little hands, put it right on my head, and began to pray. She began to pray quietly with sounds and words I had never heard her speak before. I became overwhelmed with the presence of God. All I could do was weep.

She continued to pray for me like that for several minutes. As she did, waves of God's presence rolled over me. Then she began to move my body around all the while looking at something else, as though she was taking directions from someone. At one point she took my hand and placed it over my heart. Then she lifted both of my arms, and finally she motioned for me to get down on the floor with her; she wanted me to get on my knees. It was the strangest thing, but after each movement, I would feel God's presence increase in a new way.

The whole experience lasted for about thirty minutes, and by the end I was wrecked! It amazed me that my little baby recognized God's activity in the room before I did and that she not only experienced Him but also led me into an encounter! In the months to follow Malaika would pray for people she met all the time. She would lay her hands on people in the grocery store, walking down the street—wherever we went. One time, at the age of three, she convinced a woman in an airport to get down on her knees, and the woman wept as Malaika prayed over her. That encounter empowered her!

Every time she prayed for people, they would experience God, often through tears as they were enveloped in His presence.

My prayer is that as you read these stories, you would be led into your own encounter with Jesus. He is near and longs to break into your world right now. Just as Malaika led me into an encounter with God, may these children serve as forerunners into a new level of encounter for you. May there be a whole generation of children who lead us into new encounters with God!

A RADICAL INVITATION

S HORTLY AFTER MY husband and I married, we were ministering to a group of children near Kansas City, Missouri. My husband, Jona, had heard stories about some of the really wild things I had seen God do with children, but this was one of the first times we were able to experience it together. After two days of ministering to this particular group of children, something just exploded in the room. I don't really know how to explain it, but God was in our midst.

The presence of God became very tangible, and several children began to weep, get down on their knees, or lie on their backs. We began to pray over the kids and invite the Holy Spirit to do whatever He wanted to do. Many of the children began to have visions and were dramatically being touched by God. It was like holy chaos had broken out all over the room. Not really having much of a grid for what to do in these moments, I just wanted to make space for God to do whatever He wanted. I quietly went around the room, knelt down next to each child who was experiencing something, and whispered in his or her ear, "Are you doing OK? Are you crying because you're experiencing God or because you're scared?"

Every time the response was the same. They were just overwhelmed by God's goodness and love. God was powerfully moving on a few of the children in a way that made some people feel uncomfortable. A few of the children were lying on the ground wailing and shaking violently. In all honesty it made me a little uncomfortable. I was thinking, "Oh, my gosh, parents are going to come in here and wonder what I've done to their kids! They're going to freak out!"

The beauty of what was happening was that it was so undeniably God. The presence of God was so intense in the room. I spent more than two hours just sitting and watching one little seven-year-old girl lie on the ground, shaking under the power of God, weeping at times and laughing at times. She was having the most profound encounter. She was completely in another world. By this point the other children had left, and the girl's parents were sitting next to me, praying over her. They were waiting, not wanting to interrupt this sovereign encounter.

After about two and a half hours this little girl began to quiet down. It took awhile before she could begin to talk because she was still shaking from her experience. It was as though she was glowing—you could just see God all over her. She began to tell us a very long, detailed account of what had taken place. It was so detailed and intricate, and she was so visibly touched, there is no way a child could ever make up something like that.

It all started when she prayed a little prayer: "Jesus, will You take me to heaven?" She said the next thing she saw was a wave runner, and the Lord told her to jump on. She did. From there she saw herself soaring up into another realm. She saw herself in heaven. She began to describe with her simple vocabulary what she saw. "First on this side, I saw a big thing of water, like an ocean, that looked like it was made of glass."

The Lord told her to get in the water with Him. He spent time "washing" her and talking with her about things He was washing away from her—pains, hurts, and sins. Then He baptized her. From there she explained in great detail an endless number of things she saw, heard, smelled, and experienced. Each item was so incredible and profound, we all sat there in amazement just listening. She described heaven like an old scholar who had studied the Scriptures for years.

After her incredible time of healing, deliverance, and baptism, the Lord told her He had a beautiful and holy calling for her life. He poured oil over her head and anointed her. Then He told her, "I want to show you something." He took her up to the top of a mountain ridge. From there she could see a great nation. The Lord began to share many mysteries and details about this land and its people. He talked with her about the government, the suffering of the people, and the economy. Although she was high up on the mountain, she would suddenly be able to see what the Lord was talking with her about. As He was speaking, her sight would zoom in, and she would be able to see inside a room, an orphanage, a hospital, government offices, and so on.

She said this was when she began to cry so hard because the things she saw broke her heart. The language she was using to explain the political and cultural events that were occurring was foreign to a child of this age. It was as if someone had plugged her into an encyclopedia or that she had just graduated with a political science degree. I wish you could have seen the look on her parents' faces. The Lord showed her so many specific things about this land, what was happening there, how to pray, and what He wanted to do there.

For more than two hours she was shown the mysteries of this land and heard God's heart for this place. The Lord told her, "I'm going to pour out My spirit in this land again, and one day I'm going to send you there. Right now your job is to pray about all these things I've shown you, and when the time is right, I will send you." In this experience the Lord commissioned her (at seven years old) and told her to prepare herself, because one day God would use her mightily in that land.

At that point she looked up at us and said, "He actually told me the name of the country, but I've never heard it before, so I don't know if it's real." We were all eager to know which country God had shown this child for more than two hours, the land her heart was now broken over, the land He commissioned her to bring transformation to. She hesitated. Then she said, "Have you ever heard of a place called North Korea?"

Without even knowing that a place called North Korea existed, this little girl was given the most accurate revelation of how to pray for the government, the people, the needs, the land, and for revival. It is as Matthew 11:25 says, "At that time Jesus said, 'I praise you, Father, Lord of heaven and earth, because you have hidden these things from the wise and learned, and revealed them to little children.'"

A BUTTERFLY, A BREAKTHROUGH, AND ANGELS

N 2003 I had the incredible opportunity to go into South Sudan. Officials from the south escorted my team into the nation to reach out to the thousands of children and youth whose lives had been devastated by years of gruesome war. Because this was before the peace agreement of 2005, conditions were still very hostile, and the level of fear and despair was unlike anything I had ever witnessed before.

Some of the senior leaders of South Sudan's makeshift government were Christians, and they invited us in to share the gospel with thousands of their children and youth. It was an amazing opportunity. My heart was instantly overwhelmed for these kids. Many of them had lost a parent or both parents in the war. Everything that once existed for them was no more. I was shown the remains of what used to be a hospital, a school, a village. I heard stories that would rip your heart out—children living in caves, people constantly having to run for their lives, constant attacks, fear, destruction, death.

As one generation went to war to defend their religious freedom, another was left to raise and defend themselves alone, and many had never even heard the gospel that many of their parents died to defend. I felt like I was walking on holy ground. We partnered with an indigenous group that started makeshift schools under trees. Thousands of children were meeting under these appointed trees in an attempt to receive some sort of education in the midst of war. During the days we would travel to these different locations, each day meeting hundreds of new children. Many children received Christ, were healed, and experienced Jesus's love for the first time. It was beautiful!

Because of some flooding that was taking place, one day we were not able to reach the designated location to meet the children. The river had literally overtaken the road we needed to cross, so we had to return to our base. The next day we received word that more than several hundred, possibly a thousand, children had been waiting near the big mango tree where we were supposed to meet them the day before. The message we received was that the children had been told that someone was coming to explain to them the truth about who God was, so they waited and waited and were refusing to leave until they heard this message.

Now, you can only imagine what that did to my heart. These precious babies had been sitting under a tree for almost two days desperate to hear a message of hope that could save them from their living hell. The next day was our last day in Sudan, and we had to cross the border into Uganda to catch a flight. After losing many hours on the side of the washed-out road, our driver finally decided to attempt to cross the river. Nervous and very prayerful, because water was up to our windows, we inched our way across the river and, thankfully, were able to continue on our way.

Our plan was to stop to visit these children as we headed

toward the border. We had been given strict instructions to cross by 5:00 p.m., or our safety could not be guaranteed. Unfortunately, our river wading pushed us way behind schedule, and we had just enough time to rush to the border. All I could think about was those precious children sitting under that tree in the blazing heat for two days, desperate to know Jesus. Although others in our group thought we should focus on making our plane, I knew we absolutely needed to stop. I finally convinced our driver to stop for the children for just a few minutes.

As we pulled into the area where the kids were waiting, children surrounded our car, waving branches and singing with such joy. They saw us coming from far off and were ecstatic that we had finally arrived. We were speechless. As we got out of the car, the children gave us gifts and eggs to eat, and they sang songs they had prepared for us. We shared the good news with them that day, and as far as I could tell, every single one raised his hand, eager to receive Christ. Our five minutes turned into something closer to an hour, but it was one of the best hours of my life. Children living in one of the darkest places on earth found the light. Needless to say, our hearts were full and their hearts were full, and God sovereignly protected us as we crossed the border.

A Butterfly Miracle

While in Sudan I also witnessed something very challenging that I had never experienced before. Not all of the children we shared Christ with were as eager to receive Him as this particular group. Every day while we were in the nation, we ministered to a group of older children between the ages of thirteen to eighteen. In all honesty, in most places I had traveled to, most of the children and youth I encountered wanted to give their lives to Jesus. Not these teenagers, though.

We spent three hours every evening preaching the gospel, sharing testimonies, praying for the sick, and inviting this group of youth to embrace God's gift for them. Day after day, not one would get saved. I was baffled. I could tell they were experiencing God; their eyes were so full of desire for what I was talking about. You could have heard a pin drop in the room—they were listening so intently to every word I said.

Each night as I extended them an invitation to give their lives to Jesus, they sat frozen, holding back tears. It was so overwhelming that I began to weep right there in front of them. I could feel their pain. I could feel their fear. They understood that becoming a Christian might cost them their life because government forces from North Sudan were indiscriminately killing Christians in the south. These teens did nothing impulsively. Each day, after three hours of ministering to them, praying for them, and loving on them, I would dismiss the meeting. No one moved. They would sit there in silence long after I left.

One day as I was preparing my message, I felt the Lord wanted me to talk about the beauty and power of being a new creation. Thinking about the fact that I had been given three hours to fill, I was looking for some type of visual aid for my sermon. I instantly thought about a butterfly. A butterfly is such a great picture of a new creation. It starts off as a caterpillar, stuck to the ground, getting stepped on, overlooked, and so limited in what it can do or where it can go.

After it undergoes a process of transformation, it becomes one of our most loved creatures—the beautiful butterfly.

The regal butterfly is adorned with beauty, loved by all, and free to fly. It is beautiful and free—just as we are all created to be. When we receive the work of the cross in our lives, we are transformed, we are made beautiful, and we are given the gift of freedom. So finding a butterfly for my illustration seemed like a really great idea. The only problem was, it was pouring rain. Butterflies usually don't hang around when it's raining. I hoped the rain would end soon, but it only increased. By the time our meeting started, it was pouring rain and very dark. Although I kept feeling as though God wanted to tell these kids He would make them a new creation, take their pain, make them beautiful, remove their chains, and give them freedom, I knew my chances of finding a butterfly were slim to none.

We headed to the meeting and got settled, and as I stood up to preach, I placed my Bible on the podium. I opened my Bible to the passage I would speak out of, 2 Corinthians 5:17, "Therefore, if anyone is in Christ, he is a new creation; old things have passed away; behold, all things have become new" (NKJV).

I looked up at the kids, and just as I was about to start speaking, one of the most amazing things happened. From the open door in the very back of the room I saw a huge butterfly (or it may have been a large colored moth) fly into the room. It flew from the back of the room, over the heads of all the kids, right up to where I was, and landed on my open Bible. It literally was sitting on 2 Corinthians 5. The whole room gasped. The kids were very intrigued and wanted to see the butterfly. I was so excited! God is just so much fun. In the midst of the pouring rain He sent in this beautiful butterfly.

It was pearly white with the most vibrant colors on its wings. It was about the size of my hand, and it just sat there on my Bible. I was thinking to myself, "If people don't get saved tonight, I don't know what I'm going to do!" Well, for three hours I shared about being a new creation. The entire time that butterfly just sat on my Bible and never moved. I even picked up my Bible and walked around the room, showing everyone. The butterfly just continued to sit there. It truly was amazing.

At the end of the night I gave another invitation for salvation. The children were choking back tears. Some stared at the floor and some looked deep into my eyes, silently begging to have what I was talking about, but no one would accept the invitation to receive Christ. Not one. I could not contain myself. I wept, telling them through my sobs how good God was, how safe He was, how much He loved them, how they could trust Him. Many others cried as well, but they just weren't ready. When I finished, the beautiful butterfly got up and gracefully began to fly away. It flew out just as it had come in, and it disappeared into the night.

I was in turmoil all night long. I tossed and turned in my humble little bed, praying, crying, and praying some more. These kids desperately needed to encounter God. They were living in so much pain, and the cost was so high for them. Very early in the morning I heard a knock on the little door to my hut. I opened the door to find a young man I'll call Jumo.[1]

Jumo was sixteen years old, and he also had been in turmoil all night. He apologized for the very early visit but told me he could not wait another moment. He shared how he and several other students had not left the building from the night before. He said they just sat in silence, contemplating what I had said and warring within themselves, considering the cross and God's gift of becoming a new creation.

He looked intensely into my eyes and with great seriousness said, "I am ready to die for Jesus Christ. I am ready to become His slave." Jumo got down on his knees right there and began to weep as I prayed with him, and he received God's gift of salvation. I spent some more time ministering to Jumo, and he left my porch at around 7:00 a.m. By 9:00 a.m. Jumo had already led two of his classmates to Jesus. He showed up later that morning to introduce me to his first two converts. What joy! Within two hours he had already led two others to the Lord.

A BREAKTHROUGH FOR MARY

It happened to be pouring down rain that early morning, and shortly after Jumo left, there was another knock on my door. Wondering if Jumo was back, I opened it to find one of the teachers from the nearby school where the youth we had been ministering to lived in a large dorm. The school was very simple, and the dorms the students lived in were even simpler—mud buildings, dirt floors, thatched roofs, and an occasional little window. There was a dorm for boys and one for girls. Each of the dorms held about seventy-five students. All of the students we had been preaching the gospel to in the evenings lived in these dorms.

The teacher was frantic and said, "Please, Sister Jennifer, you must come immediately! One of the girls is possessed by a demon, and all of the girls are terrified." I rallied my team, and we dressed quickly and headed over to the girls' dorm. Because of the rain everything was muddy and soppy. As we approached the entrance, I saw a young girl lying facedown just inside the entrance. I'll call her Mary.[2] She was a thin girl, and she was lying there, eyes rolled back, growling and convulsing. All the other girls were squished up against the walls with looks of horror on their faces. Just to get my bearings, I took a deep breath and whispered the name "Jesus." Instantly Mary's body was picked up and thrown several feet in the other direction and was now facing up.

Now lying on her back with her arms over her head, Mary began to be dragged out of the building backward as though someone was pulling her by the wrists. All the girls started screaming and crying, and I got really mad at the enemy.

God had been beautifully putting His love on display for these youth, and the enemy was trying to make a scene and distract these kids from God. Two of the local pastors helped me to grab her legs and stop her from being dragged around. At that point we began to pray over Mary, speaking to her spirit and silencing the enemy. Mary began to fade in and out. In the moments when she was present, I spoke to her about her situation. I told her that we could cast this demon out, but her safety and freedom were in Jesus. If she didn't surrender to Jesus and come under His covering, this demon would likely just return and be even worse.

You could see her inner struggle. She would become more present as she contemplated the idea, then when fear would set in, we'd lose her again. This went on for quite some time. I kept speaking over her, "Mary, Jesus is the one who can set you free." After many anguishing moments, all the girls huddled against the wall began to yell out, "Do it, Mary! Just accept Jesus! You'll be free! Do it, Mary!" All the girls who had not received Christ themselves were begging their friend to do so because they knew Jesus had the power to set her free.

Finally Mary let go of her fears and told me she wanted Jesus. We prayed a simple prayer together, and instantly Mary was completely delivered. As soon as we prayed, every demonic manifestation left. She became fully aware of where she was and what was going on, and she looked like a completely different person. All of her friends were now crying with joy, hugging one another and thanking God. The teacher took Mary to get cleaned up, as she was covered in mud, and a short time later Mary returned in the brightest yellow dress you ever saw and a huge grin on her face.

I honestly did not even recognize her. She could not stop smiling. She joined us back in the girls' dorm and shared her story. She had been tormented by this demon since she was a young child when her parents had taken her to the witch doctor. She had lived with a dark feeling inside of her for years. She rejoiced, telling us that she felt completely different, completely free, completely happy, completely new! Jesus had fixed everything in a moment. Mary and I were able to lead the majority of her classmates in the dorm that day to Jesus. They not only saw the butterfly, but they also saw Mary become the butterfly.

Mary and Jumo were both on fire for Jesus. They gathered other students together to pray and seek God. They shared their faith and the power of their testimonies with all of their classmates. I wanted so much to stay longer in Sudan and spend time helping them grow in their walk with God. When it was time for us to leave the country, my heart was so heavy in intercession for those kids who had encountered the love of their Father but were still trapped in a war zone. I immediately started making plans to send in a small team to remain in the area long term to continue pouring into the kids and partner with what God was doing there.

I was devastated to find out that right after we left, fighting increased in the region and our main contact had to flee the country because government forces were hunting him down. No one was being allowed in. I was in Canada when I received the message, and when I heard the news, I just began to cry. God had started such a beautiful work with all of the children and youth in South Sudan, and I didn't want to abandon them. Who was going to disciple them? Who was going to encourage them?

That night I lay in bed praying fervently that God would send angels to minister to the kids. If nobody else could be there, God certainly could send angels to be with the children. That was my prayer over the next several weeks. About a month later I received an e-mail from one of the teachers at the school. He had been able to travel into Uganda, which is where he was when he contacted me.

This teacher was writing to let me know that God was doing a beautiful and incredible work through the kids at the school. Mary and Jumo were still leading the troops, and many students had received Christ and were experiencing Him in powerful ways. He was most excited to inform me that many of the students had experienced a corporate angelic encounter. At the same time they all saw huge angels standing in the middle of the school courtyard. They were so encouraged and comforted because they knew the angels were there to protect them and minister to them. He wanted to let me know God was continuing to encounter the children powerfully.

God sent angels to the kids, and they were strengthened by their encounter! I fell in love with God a million times over again. God wants to encounter us too. He is so good and so faithful. He knows exactly what we need, exactly when we need it.

5
A DATE WITH JESUS

I MET MEGAN AT a summer camp when she was five years old. Each summer I would return to the same place in Canada to minister to a group of children from all over the region. During one of my sessions with the older kids I began to challenge them to start "dating" God. Jokingly I suggested that if they spent as much time "dating" God as they did talking with their friends about the boy or girl they liked, they would have an awesome breakthrough in their walk with the Lord. I challenged them to set aside time to spend alone with God—and to make it special and really get to know Him. I wouldn't find this out until the next year when I returned, but Megan took my challenge very seriously. This is what unfolded.

Megan, who at age five was too young for my class, decided to come anyway with her older brother. She sat next to him during the class and was deeply stirred by the idea of going on a date with God. She decided that when she returned home, she would give it a try. After thinking and planning for a while, she informed her parents that she was going to have a special date with Jesus that day. Her parents supported her endeavor and let her continue with her plan.

Her parents soon realized how serious she was because she had cleaned her room, totally unsolicited, in preparation of her date. (Parents, you know something supernatural is happening if your child cleans her room without being asked!) She then took a bath and put on her best dress. She asked her mother if she could use real food and a candle for the date. Her mother thought that was a little extreme, but she allowed her to place an unlit candle on the table. She would have to make do with using pretend food.

Disappointed but confident that Jesus wouldn't mind, Megan began to set up her little table in her room. She decorated the table, paying attention to every detail, wanting it to be perfect for Jesus. After everything was in place, she went out to her family and told them to please not disturb her because she was going to have a very special date with Jesus in her room. She went up into her room, sat down at her little table, and, full of faith, waited for Jesus to come.

One year later, standing next to her mom at the same summer camp, her eyes huge, she told us the story: "And that is when I heard a knock on the door." This day would unlock a whole new realm in Megan's life. This shy little five-year-old girl saw Jesus walk into her room.

Megan said Jesus sat down at her little table in the spot she had lovingly prepared for Him. He smiled at her, and she was so excited and drawn to Him. When I asked her, "Can you explain to me what you mean by you saw Jesus come into your room?" She said, "I could see Him very clearly. It was like I could see the room as it was, and I could see Him there at the same time." It was as though she was looking through two lenses at the same time.

She proceeded to describe her very sweet time with Jesus. She said they talked and talked and that He didn't mind that the food was pretend. I asked her, "Well, what did you guys talk about?" Her response was perfect! She said, "Oh, you know, all the normal stuff people talk about. He talked about stuff going on in heaven. I talked about stuff going on with me. We took turns talking about things we like or don't like. It was really fun!"

She remembered being very aware of how she was holding her fork (pinky up, of course!) and how she just wanted everything to be perfect for Jesus. She continued to share with me about that special encounter she had. She told me that after dinner Jesus invited her to come out to the backyard because He had a special surprise for her. The look in her eyes spoke louder than her words as she told me the rest of the experience.

When she arrived in the backyard, she said she saw a big, beautiful carriage that looked much like a chariot, and Jesus opened the door for her to jump in. The open-top carriage had sparkles and was drawn by two beautiful white horses. Jesus helped her in, and they began to go on an incredible ride. She described a variety of images and colors she saw as she suddenly was taken in the spirit. She was flying over different places and seeing many things—it was challenging for her to communicate in words exactly what she saw during this time. Jesus was next to her the whole time and explaining to her everything she was seeing.

He talked with her about these different places, His heart for them, and what He was doing there. He shared many special things with her. She recalls it being a fun and playful time with Him. She told me that at one point they stopped, got out, and jumped around in a puddle, just laughing and playing together. Although it was a puddle, she said it also looked like a flowing stream. Finally they returned to the backyard, and Jesus gave her a sweet little kiss on the cheek and told her He loved spending time with her and that He would love to have another date with her again soon.

Megan's mother was standing beside her daughter as she excitedly told me all about her date with Jesus. The mom's joy and gratitude shone on her face. When Megan was finished telling me all about her experience, her mother pulled me aside and wanted to tell me her side of it all. She was clearly deeply touched as she tried to communicate the impact this had had on her daughter. She explained how Megan had always been so shy and quiet around strangers and that this encounter had dramatically impacted her daughter.

She told me she and her husband were shocked by the level of revelation their daughter showed as she explained some of the things Jesus told her. Their five-year-old was using words they had never heard her say before, and she was explaining complex spiritual concepts to them that they knew she had never in her life been exposed to or heard. In Megan's mind she was simply sharing with them pieces of her conversation with Jesus, but this five-year-old girl was marked by her encounter with Jesus!

Megan's mother said that day impacted her daughter so significantly that she became less shy. She began to share her faith with others and speak up at her church, sharing some of the treasures God had spoken to her. The whole family was provoked by the encounter and the dramatic changes they saw in her. Her mother told me, "Even her little brother has had trips to heaven now. Our whole family is experiencing God in powerful ways!"

I love this story. I love it for so many reasons. A child—a sweet, big-brown-eyed little girl—wasn't afraid to put her love and hunger on display for God. She "drew near" the best way she knew how, even if it seemed silly. Her hunger and simplicity not only led her into an encounter with the divine, but they also broke open a door for her whole family to experience God in a deeper way. When you encounter God in a real and personal way, in a way that goes past mere intellectual consent, you will be forever changed.

Isaiah 55:11 says, "My word, which comes from my mouth, is like the rain and snow. It will not come back to me without results, but it will accomplish whatever I want and achieve whatever I send it to do" (GW). When we hear God's "word"—His heart, His thoughts, etc.—and when we experience the essence of who He is, it changes us. We are constantly being transformed through our experiences and encounters with God.

Megan is now thirteen years old and more in love with Jesus than ever. I had the honor of interviewing her about what her relationship with Jesus looks like now.[1] She explained to me that when she had that first "date" with Jesus at age five, she started to "understand stuff." Experiencing God like that didn't seem "extraordinary"; it was "normal fun," "just like another play date."

As time went on, Megan continued to "meet with God" in so many really special ways. She recounted times of eating lunch with Him or seeing herself dancing with Him in a beautiful ballroom. Many times in the past four or five years, when she "soaks" in prayer, she'll see a cup that looks something like a wine glass. The liquid inside the glass never runs out, and the more she drinks it, the happier she gets.

She explained that the liquid inside the cup is liquid joy, and the more you drink it, the happier you feel. Whenever she drinks from that cup, she is overwhelmed with a supernatural joy that cannot be explained. She will just burst out laughing, "not normal laughing—loud, long laughing, and I just can't stop! The joy is just overwhelming, and whenever I drink from that cup, I'm left in such a happy and giggly mood."

She said sometimes after drinking from that cup she will hug somebody, and then for no apparent reason they will start laughing too. She loves that she has been able to partake of this kind of joy and sees it as a gift since her middle name is Joy.

A HEAVENLY GARDEN

Megan has grown accustomed to just "hanging out" with God and has truly cultivated a relationship with Him in her life. She told me how one night recently she was having trouble falling asleep, so she decided to "just hang out" with God. She closed her eyes and waited for His presence. She saw what looked like large curtains in front of her. She walked through the curtains. Instantly she was wearing a gorgeous gown that looked much like the dress Belle wore in the Disney film *Beauty and the Beast*, but in pink instead of gold.

Megan saw the Lord standing there waiting for her beside a fiery chariot. She stepped into the chariot, and He drove her to a beautiful enclosed garden. The garden was hedged in on all sides and had a beautiful arched doorway. The garden was divided into four rooms, and at first glance it didn't look too big. But as they entered, all of a sudden Megan realized this amazing garden went on for miles, and she couldn't even see the other end.

As they entered into the first room, Megan could see rows and rows of fruits and vegetables, every fruit and vegetable imaginable. She picked a handful of strawberries and peas, because that was what she was in the mood for, and together they carried them back to the chariot and set them inside. Next they walked into the second room of the garden. In this room she could see a huge rolling hill covered with the most beautiful flowers. She picked an armful of flowers, and they carried them back to the chariot.

Then they went into the third room, which was full of all different types of trees. Jesus asked her which was her favorite, and she picked out a beautiful apple tree that was in full bloom. The Lord walked over to the tree and touched it, and it seemed to just disappear. Then she realized that in His hand was an apple seed, and together they carried it back to the chariot and placed it inside.

Finally they headed to the fourth room, which was full of flowing, grassy hills. Megan explained that the grass was thick like carpet but with the softest texture you've ever felt. They were lying in the grass and enjoying its softness when Megan noticed the Lord was doing something. She sat up to get a better look and saw that He had stuck His fingers under the grass and was rolling up a piece as you would roll up sod. They carried the piece of rolled-up grass back to the chariot and placed it inside with all the other items. Then together they got back into the chariot and flew out of the garden.

Within a moment they were landing on a beautiful cloud way up high. The Lord helped her out of the chariot, and then He reached in and grabbed the rolled-up grass and unrolled it on top of the cloud. He took the apple seed and dropped it into the grass; all of a sudden the same beautiful apple tree from the garden stood there in full bloom in the grass. Megan was amazed by what she saw.

Next He took the flowers she had lovingly selected and placed them as a centerpiece where they were to sit. Last, He pulled out the strawberries and peas, and they sat together on that little slice of heaven on the cloud having a wonderful picnic and enjoying each other's company. Megan felt so loved and cared for by the Lord.

Suddenly, the vision shifted, and Megan was again standing in front of the large curtains. Not wanting the encounter to end, she walked back through the curtains, and instantly she saw herself back in this spiritual place on the cloud with the Lord. This time she was wearing a dazzling blue Cinderella-style dress that had beautiful puffed sleeves. In front of her she could see the Lord standing next to a huge red carpet, which had angels standing at each corner. The Lord helped her onto the carpet, and instantly the angels picked up the corners, and they began flying through time and space.

Megan was enjoying every moment of this incredible adventure, but more than anything she just loved being next to Jesus. The carpet came to a stop at a glistening pool. Megan instantly recognized the pool because it was a place she had visited before with Jesus. But the Lord simply shook His head and said, "This won't do," and once again they were soaring through the air. They eventually landed at a beautiful, pristine beach. Megan began to walk in the sand and was amazed by its incredibly soft texture. She walked with Jesus into the water, and they were enjoying its beauty together.

Then the Lord reached down into the water and pulled out a beautiful shell. With so much delight on His face, He gave the shell to Megan and told her to put it up to her ear. When she put the shell up to her ear, she was expecting to hear the ocean, but instead all she could hear was the Lord's voice saying over and over again, "I love you. I love you. I love you." Those words, that truth, went deep into her spirit; then suddenly she was standing back at the curtains.

So moved by this love, she pushed through the curtains once again, and instantly she was returned to this place with the Lord. Suddenly her clothing shifted, and she was wearing a brilliant green dress that had a golden M on it. This time the Lord was waiting for her next to a large, sparkling green carriage. A large, transparent, glistening horse with wings that looked like glass was drawing the carriage. Amazed by the beauty of the horse and carriage, Megan stepped into the carriage, wondering where the Lord would take her this time. Suddenly they were flying again, and before long they landed at the base of cave.

Together with the Lord, she began to walk through the cave. Right away she noticed the cave had an incredible echo, so she joyfully started singing a song. The Lord joined in and started singing with her in the cave. The sounds she heard were unexplainable; they were the most breathtakingly beautiful sounds she had ever heard. She was overtaken by the Lord's voice. She explains, "His voice, it's so full, so strong. It makes you feel so good. His singing voice, it's hard to believe. It's even better than His talking voice."

After Megan soaked in the power and the beauty of the Lord's voice, He began to lead her deep into this tunnel. Megan was delighted to see that the tunnel walls were gleaming. Embedded into the walls were countless diamonds. She was in a diamond mine. He handed her a pick, and together they started hacking away at the wall. He chipped away two stunning pink heart-shaped gems and gave them to her. She was able to chip away a beautiful green-colored gem and gave it to the Lord in return. Last, the Lord chipped out a rainbow-colored gem that was unlike anything Megan had ever seen before. He held onto it, and once again Megan found herself standing at the large curtains.

Amazed by what she was seeing and filled with so much love for this friend of hers, Megan pushed herself one last time through the curtain to be near the Lord. This time she was wearing a slim pink dress that had brilliant gems on it. And there He was. The Lord was standing there with a smile on His face, waiting for her with so much joy. He was standing next to an upside-down rainbow. She quickly jumped onto the rainbow, so eager to just be with Him, and instantly the rainbow drew them away.

They flew to a huge castle. When they arrived at the castle, an angel was holding the green gem they found in the mine. The angel flew up and set it perfectly on the peak of the castle. Almost instantly light hit the gem, and it radiated beautiful color and light in all directions. "It was kind of like a disco ball but better!" she explained.

A joyous party broke out at the castle. Everywhere Megan looked angels were dancing and playing. Other angels were playing music. It was just such a celebration! Megan felt so alive and so happy in this place. She was enjoying every moment of this encounter, trying to drink in every wonderful thing she was experiencing. There was so much joy in this place; there was so much love there. Finally the Lord handed her a gift to keep. He gave her a little purple purse. When she opened the purse, it projected the words "I love you," like some kind of futuristic device you might see in a Batman movie.

The encounter ended there, and Megan lay in her bed amazed, overwhelmed, and so grateful. She pondered everything she had seen and realized that all of it—every experience, every gift—was centered around His love for her. It was all about Him expressing His perfect love for her and her gaining a deep revelation of that love. Everything that happened was about Him saying, "I love you."

She felt different. How can you experience love like that and not be transformed? In my times of talking with Megan I could see how confident she is in the love God has for her. This wasn't just head knowledge. This was a true, living experience. She knows the love of God. It has marked her. It has made her who she is, and the way she lives is evidence of that. She made the statement, "Sometimes I just get so mad when people believe God is responsible for bad things. How can a God who loves us so very much ever do that?" Megan has encountered the love of God—she has tasted it, she has experienced it, and it now defines her.

What a beautiful experience—Megan making herself available and Jesus wooing her in relationship. May we all learn how to just "pass through the curtain," stop living in the flesh and dwell in the Spirit, and in that place be absolutely transformed by God's love.

ENJOYING GOD'S PRESENCE

While I was interviewing Megan and trying to dig out some of the specific revelation Jesus shared with her, she made a statement that I loved, because it was so wise and powerful. She said: "I don't spend time with Jesus because I'm looking for some kind of 'revelation.' Our times together aren't about me trying to seek out some big mystery. Our time together is simply about enjoyment. We just love to be together. When God is trying to get something across to me, He comes into my world. But when I go into His world, I don't really pray, 'God, come.' I just close my eyes and picture His face smiling at me—and then it just happens quickly. My only motive is to just spend time with Him and play and have fun and enjoy Him. I guess, somehow, when it's all done, I just know things, but that is not my focus."

She went on to tell me how as she has grown older, God has continued to speak to her and meet with her in ways that have helped her through some of the challenges she has faced in life. She explained that sometimes she has struggles with self-image and comparing herself with others. But one time she had an encounter that shifted her perspective. Here's her story of what happened.

> One day I went up to heaven, and I saw myself standing by a pool. I was wearing a beautiful pink princess dress. My hair was in a beautiful fancy bun, and I just burst out, "Oh, that's so beautiful!" God was standing next to me and did something I never expected. He grabbed my hand and jumped into the pool. I didn't understand. I was drenched. "My beautiful dress!" I thought. My pretty bun was soaking wet and starting to fall out. I didn't understand why He did that. Then He took my hand, and we started walking down a long, dry, dusty, dirt path. The loose dust started to cling to my wet dress, and soon my dress was covered in mud.
>
> The path we were walking on led us into this forest;

then the path seemed to disappear. The forest was dense, and twigs were pulling out my bun and ripping up my dress. Finally He walked me out to a clearing. Everything I thought was beautiful—my hair, my dress—was destroyed. He looked me in the eyes. His eyes had that "happy essence" they always have, but I knew He was serious. He looked at me lovingly and said, "You are beautiful!" His words had such a weight to them—it's like the essence of His voice is honesty. When He says something, you just can't argue with it. It's undeniable truth. Ever since that day, if I ever start thinking about my looks, I just look into the mirror, and I can still hear Him say, "You are beautiful!"[2]

God is so kind and understanding of what each of us needs—at just the right moment. What if every young girl could have a revelation of who she is before she trudges through the teenage years? God is so personal and tender. We all need to hear Him speak over us, "You are beautiful!" It's not all the outward things that make us pleasing to God—our acts, our service, our sacrifice. When all those things have been torn and destroyed through the journey, it is simply who we are that is so beautiful.

One of the reasons I wanted to share a little bit about Megan's journey is because from a young age she has cultivated a real and authentic relationship with Jesus. She is just a very normal little girl who has made herself available to encounter the Lord, and she has cultivated and nurtured that place of encounter in her life. Her parents have seen such a dramatic difference in her life and have witnessed in awe the powerful fruit that has come out of their daughter's encounters with Jesus.

I spent some time talking with Isabel, Megan's mom, and she told me that many times unexpectedly, in random situations, something deep and powerful would just come out of Megan's mouth. People would be shocked and speechless when these "truth bombs" went off. Isabel knows this happens only because of Megan's very sincere personal connection with God. She has seen extraordinary fruit come out of her daughter's life as she has stayed deeply connected to God's heart.

This once very shy child now walks with such peace, love, joy, and authority. Isabel told me that in the midst of some really painful situations that were happening, she watched Megan choose forgiveness and love. She knows her response is absolutely only because of her connection to God. The maturity and perspective she is able to respond with is simply supernatural—it's just not natural outside of God.

Isabel told me of another experience Megan had around the age of seven. During a kids' club program, Megan got a dazed look on her face, and Isabel knew she was having an experience with the Holy Spirit. After her encounter this seven-year-old girl told her mom in great detail about a planet she saw. It was dirty and broken and sad. Then all of a sudden God took a huge paintbrush and just started painting—everywhere, all over the planet, painting, painting, painting, and making it beautiful. He kept saying, "This is My world! I'm making it beautiful!"

Isabel said these kinds of experiences have marked Megan. They have taught her to see pain and brokenness from heaven's perspective. It has trained her to see with eyes of hope and faith. I love the revelation from this encounter—God is making the world beautiful again! I pray that all of us, like Megan, can have the eyes to see what God is doing and the faith to partner with Him to accomplish it.

I asked Isabel what kind of advice she could offer parents who want to encourage their children to experience God in deep ways. Her response was simple. "You have to live that relationship yourself first." She explained that as parents, you have to cultivate hunger in your own life, model it for your kids, pursue Him all the time in the day-to-day activities, and stay in the place of thinking, "He is my answer. He is what I long for."

She added that it is also important to give your kids the opportunity to fail. Isabel has five children, and all of them, like Megan, have sincere relationships with the Lord. I have so much respect for this family and am so blessed by the love they are committed to cultivating with God.

I was so very blessed during my talks with Megan. I could just feel the presence of Jesus all over her. I asked her how her encounters with Jesus have changed her, and she said, "I can't say who I would be without God. I've never seen myself differently. God has always been faithful to lovingly show me when I walk off the path. He'll say, 'No, Megan, this isn't you.'"

The fruit is evident. Megan knows who she is. She is confident in the Father's love for her. Megan told me about her love for art and how she feels called to help people understand God's love. She explains, "I think that's why I experience it the way I do. I love when people 'get it,' when they understand God is saying, 'You are a prince! You are a princess!'" The joy and the love of heaven radiate out of each of Megan's words.

I asked Megan if she would graciously pray for all of you reading this book and impart the revelation of the love of the Father over you. Here it is:

God, I pray that You would bless the people reading the book, that they would come to understand that You love them and want to have fun with them. And that You are good and will never stop loving them. Amen.

Megan all dressed up and full of joy

6
WHEN GOD SHOWS UP

D URING A SEASON when my husband and I were doing quite a lot of children's ministry, we had a really cool experience that challenged us to press in to encounter God. We both were awakened in the middle of the night to see our whole room glowing and full of angels dancing with colors swirling around them. It was seriously one of the craziest things I have ever experienced, and my husband and I saw it together. The whole thing lasted for about ten seconds; then the angels and the colors disappeared. When I finally was able to fall back asleep, I continued to see the same angels dancing and singing in my dreams.

They were singing about the power and spiritual meaning of colors. I woke up hearing the last line of a song, "Orange, orange, orange is the color of visitation." When I got up in the morning, I knew God was preparing us for visitation, and I knew He wanted to encounter the children in our upcoming events.

During several of our weeklong summer conferences, children were hearing God's voice, they were feeling God's presence, and many were healed and filled with the Holy Spirit. We taught the kids to pray for and press in to encounter God. I knew that if they had just one encounter with God, their lives would be forever changed. The presence of God began to roll in the room like waves of the ocean. It was so powerful. Kids were overwhelmed by the love of God. Many of them experienced deep inner healing and physical healing. All over the room kids were crying, and several children saw visions that would mark them for life.

In one meeting where several of the children were having really powerful encounters, one little boy became very discouraged because he wasn't seeing or experiencing anything. We encouraged the kids to not compare themselves with anyone else because we all experience God differently. Because the little boy was so concerned about not encountering Jesus as the other children were, his mom decided to sit in the session to encourage him.

During the session the child leaned over to his mom very excitedly and told her, "I just saw a blue angel!" When she asked what the angel was doing, he told her, "I saw lots of sad faces in the room, and the angel was going around the room and touching each sad face. When it touched a face, the sad face would turn into a happy face!"

He was so excited by his vision he could hardly contain himself. His mother encouraged him to come and tell us what he was seeing. Upon hearing his testimony, we asked him to help us pray and release this blue angel in the room. He shared with the other children what he saw, and we began to pray that God would release this blue angel to do whatever it had come to do. I could never in a million years have guessed what was going to happen next!

I'm not sure how else to explain it, but it was like an entire room of kids started going through crazy deliverance. Several kids instantly fell to the ground wailing, crying, and shaking as though they stuck their fingers into a light socket. Several children saw images flash before them—some saw demons leaving them or things breaking off of them; they saw pain getting sucked out of their hearts and chains being broken.

Kids were crying and shaking, and this was not something these children had ever done before. Most of the children in the room had never even seen anything like that, let alone experience it. I was at a loss for what to do. I knew God was there. I didn't do this; He did. I, once again, found myself very uncomfortable with the way God was choosing to show up. I certainly wanted Him to be in our midst, but why couldn't He come in a nice little package?

I have learned a few things through the years; one is that God does things however He wants to do them. And God is famous for doing things that make the religious uncomfortable. I had to just let it go. God was clearly doing something sovereign in these kids. I didn't need to control it or even understand it.

The craziness lasted deep into the night. Many of the tears turned into ridiculous and hysterical laughing. There were children lying all over the floor, their bodies just scattered across the room. As the parents came in to get their kids, I tried my best to explain what was happening. Their children still were overwhelmed by this power encounter, and many of the parents simply had to scoop their kids up off the floor and carry them out the door.

Some of the children were roused enough to communicate, and I talked with them as they were leaving. They told me God showed them they had been carrying around pain from an abusive situation, a death, a divorce, and so forth, and Jesus took it out of them. They told me they felt completely different inside. They felt genuinely happy.

There were a few children who told me that as they lay there on the floor, they saw images of children from all over the world flash in front of them. As they saw their faces, they were filled with great compassion, and they began to intercede for children who were bound in fear and sadness. I believe God came to not only set the children there free but also to use them to unlock breakthrough for a multitude of other children!

The next morning I had no clue whether parents would bring their kids back to the weeklong summer conference we were leading. But sure enough, parents had gathered in the room and were lined up waiting to talk to me. Parent after parent told me how transformed his or her child was! They told me how their child had been bound in fear—always having nightmares, never wanting to be alone—and that for the first night ever they were happy to sleep alone in the dark. Fear was no longer ruling them. Some parents, through tears, told us they finally felt like they had their child back. Due to some traumatic event their child had been totally shut down, not himself. Personalities were restored!

It was one thing for us to hear all the stories, but it was so powerful when we were able to see the change ourselves. I remember one little boy in particular. He sat in the front row and had big buckteeth. He didn't say a word the first two days and seemed very shy, but that night that kid got massively rocked! He was one of the children on the ground shaking and going through deliverance and healing for several hours. He was a completely different child! He was suddenly talkative, smiling, interactive, happy, confident. It was amazing!

We had the privilege of returning to minister in the same place several times over the next couple of years. The testimonies of healing and freedom that came from that one night were beyond remarkable. An adopted child was freed of insecurity and never struggled with it again. Kids who had experienced sexual abuse and divorce were so completely healed and restored that their parents and counselors were shocked! God just showed up, and in one big, fat encounter set kids free from everything that bound them. He healed them and filled them with amazing joy, and everyone in their life testified to the incredible and lasting change from that one encounter! Jesus can show up, or send a blue angel, anytime He wants to!

A similar experience took place during one of the ministry times when we were in Canada. While my husband and I were praying for the kids, one little boy who couldn't have been more than seven suddenly began to see a vision. He saw himself sitting down at a table for two, and he saw Jesus sitting across from him. He asked Jesus if He would like some tea. "And that is when it all started," the little boy said. I never got the full story of what happened because after being in the encounter for more than two hours, the boy couldn't even speak. It was more than twelve hours before he was able to utter a word; God's presence was just that overwhelming. The boy's mom told me he was incredibly impacted by the visitation and, just like with the other children, God had done a deep work in him.

Even as I reflect on these stories, I continue to be amazed by the power of God and how generous He is to pour Himself out. I know some of you reading this may feel uncomfortable, alarmed, or skeptical about some of these stories. I can totally understand. I am passionate about what is authentic and pure, and in fear of looking like a crazy "charismaniac," I had to come to terms with my own discomfort with the way God moves sometimes.

The reality is, God encountered Saul like this in Acts 9. Saul's encounter was even more dramatic. He was surrounded by a bright light. He was blinded, he trembled, he fell down, and he heard a voice speaking to him. That's pretty intense. If God was so keen on encountering a murderous sinner, how much more do you think He wants to encounter His children who have been brought near through the cross and want to know Him?

I don't understand many of the things God does, but that's OK. My job is not to judge the way God moves. My job is to be a fruit inspector, and the fruit that has grown out of these children's encounters is phenomenal. God is powerful, and His power changes lives. Let us not ever forget that.

A JESUS TROPHY

After several days of ministering to a group of children during another ministry trip, I was approached by one of the moms. She wanted to tell me what God was doing in her two sons, ages six and four. The six-year-old loved sports and was really good at them. He had already won a few trophies, and it was obvious he excelled in sports.

His younger brother, who was four, had been having a hard time with his brother's success. He desperately wanted to be good at sports like his older brother, but he was still young and just not very coordinated. In all honesty, it looked as though sports was not going to be his strength. The boys' mom told me he would often cry and wanted to know when he would ever be good enough to get a trophy. Every time his brother came home with another trophy, it just seemed to add fuel to the fire and left this little four-year-old heartbroken about not having a trophy of his own.

Over the course of the week in our children's meetings, the boys had been learning how to hear God's voice, and in the evenings the family would practice hearing God together. One night as the mother tucked the two boys into bed, she encouraged them to be listening to God throughout the night. Early the next morning the younger son came running out of his room, full of excitement and joy, screaming, "I got a trophy! I got a Jesus Trophy!" He was beaming from ear to ear and was so excited.

"What do you mean?" his parents asked. The little boy began to explain that during the night he had a dream. In the dream Jesus came to him and said, "You are so great at loving people! You are a champion for love! So I'm going to give you the best trophy. You get a Jesus Trophy!" That was all this little boy needed to hear. Every ounce of insecurity was washed out of his heart, and he was so proud and excited to be the owner of a Jesus Trophy!

Isn't that beautiful? God is so perfect and so great! God encounters us in just the way we need Him to! This mother was so excited to tell me the story. She said her son was walking with pep in his step; he was so excited and blessed by Jesus.

MY WINDOW GUARDIAN

When I was two years old, I had the first encounter with Jesus I can remember. During that time our neighbors happened to have roosters. As a curious young child I probably stuck my fingers through the fence and no doubt had them pecked. Whatever the cause, I somehow developed a terrible fear that at night the roosters would come through my window and peck me when I fell asleep. Traumatizing, I know. Anyway, my fear of these pecking roosters that may come through my window left me crying in anguish many, many nights.

My parents tried everything they could to console me, explaining that roosters couldn't open windows and I would be fine, but nothing seemed to work. After several nights of them trying to console me to no avail, my parents decided they were going to have to just let me cry it out. They explained to me that if I cried, they wouldn't be coming into my room. I would just have to work it out. Well, I cried. I cried a lot. I was in full-blown fear scream crying; then instantly I stopped. My mom jumped up to check on me, thinking I was choking or something, but my dad stopped her. He told her not to go in, to just leave me alone because I was fine.

My parents knew it was very odd that I would abruptly stop crying like that. Kids usually unwind gradually then eventually fall asleep, but I just stopped mid-scream. They let me be, and early the next morning I ran out of my room and yelled, "Did you guys see Jesus?"

"What?" my parents asked. I explained to them in detail how Jesus came into my room when I was crying and that He told me I didn't need to cry because He would sit on my bed (I showed them right where He sat) and guard my window for me. I didn't need to worry. My parents were surprised and amazed, and I was as happy as could be. I never cried again about roosters coming in my window. Jesus was with me. Jesus would always guard my window.

7
CONNER'S ENCOUNTER

S OME FRIENDS OF mine have a son named Conner, who had a radical encounter with God when he was ten years old. I'll let his dad, Ben, tell you the story in his own words.

Two or three years ago Conner had an extreme encounter with God. I was on staff at the church where Conner attended school. One day I was walking by the chapel at Conner's school and heard some crazy yelling, screaming, and laughing coming from inside, so I thought I should pop in and see what was happening. What I first saw was the students and the teachers, including the principal of the school, in a circle toward the front of the chapel. Many of the children were weeping and crying out to God. Then one of the teachers came to the back and said to me, "That is your son in the middle of the group on the floor. Can you come and help us?"

I went up to the front to see my son, Conner, weeping, shaking, and writhing on the ground. At times he would groan or cry out, even scream as tears flowed out of him. One of his teachers was holding his head so he would not hit it against the floor as another wave of God's presence came over him. The intensity of the encounter was frightening. Children all around were lying on the ground, weeping and crying out to God, keeping their distance from Conner but staying close enough to touch him with the tips of their fingers. Others were just watching with concern and awe.

I lay down beside him, cradled his head, and asked how long this had been going on. The teachers replied, "Almost an hour now." Both the principal and the school's children's director asked me, "Is this God, and is he OK?" I whispered to Conner, "Is this God, and is this good?" Through tears and groans Conner nodded his head in the affirmative.

The presence increased in waves, and with each new wave Conner's body would be picked up off the ground two to three feet then come down shaking, groaning, and weeping. The next chapel with the older students was about to begin in the same room, and the teachers asked, "Should we stop this?" I said no and that we should just move him behind the stage where he would not be disturbed. For the next hour I cradled him between my legs to keep him from being physically hurt by the manifestations.

At this point things ramped up, and it became very scary for me as a dad. Conner began to display some mannerisms like those of children with developmental disorders. He started to slur and tug at his mouth with his finger. He also began to shake his head back and forth and roll his eyes as if he could not get them to focus on anything in the physical. I could tell at this point that Conner's spirit was getting farther and farther away from his physical body.

Despite my fear that he might not come out of this mental state, my continual prayer was that God would strengthen his mortal body so he would be able to receive everything God had for him. I cried out, "God, I trust You with my son. This is what we have always prayed for!" Over and over I prayed these two prayers. You see, it is one thing to press in yourself to an encounter with God that is frightening and unknown, but it is a whole other thing to hang on to an encounter of this intensity for your child. It really does test how good you believe God to be. You also have to know the only other time I had seen manifestations this intense was when someone was being delivered of demonic possession. I knew this was something else entirely—something so much more powerful and frightening.

Two full hours had past, and I was supposed to be attending a missions meeting on the same campus as my son's school. There was no one to cover for me at the time. Not wanting to end what God was doing, I carried my writhing son across the campus to the meeting and placed him in the back of the room as I ran the meeting. Needless to say, we had a powerful time in our meeting that day. As we wrapped up the meeting, Conner began to come back to himself. The tugging at his mouth started to relax, and awareness seemed to return to his eyes, as if he could see in the physical again. Then he was able to speak again, and he was intensely thirsty.

After giving him water and allowing him to rest for a bit, I asked him what had happened. Conner said the worship had been really good that day, and the presence of God had come in the room. He began to weep and fell to the floor as the weight of God's presence increased. I asked him what was happening throughout the encounter, and he was able to walk me through the experience. He said, "Dad, I saw Jesus's hand, and it had a hole in it. He laid His hand on me as I was lying on the ground. When Jesus laid His hand on me, my body would lift off the ground, and I could feel the power of God go through my whole body. And I could see it too. It was light, like white and blue lightning going through my whole body. Then my heart was lit on fire, and I could see all of my friends, and I could see whose heart was on fire and whose heart was not."

This happened during the first chapel service. Then when we moved Conner behind the stage, he said a huge black angel came to him. He said the angel looked like God in the movie *Evan Almighty*. That was the role Morgan Freeman played in the film. Conner said the angel had three arms—two at his sides like a human and a third that came out of his back and over his head.

Conner said the angel took him to a globe and told him he wanted to show him something. As the angel took the globe in his three arms, he told Conner to look, and the globe was actually the whole world. As Conner looked, he saw Africa, and as he continued to look, his vision zoomed in on Africa until he could see all of the mothers and fathers and children in the entire continent. He said they were laughing and dancing and praising God because "they were hungry no longer!" They had everything they needed.

As I carried Conner over to the missions meeting, he said he was flying and then came back to himself. At different times during the encounter Conner said he could see all of us but that he was somewhere else at the same time and could also see the other things. He said that at times he felt very far away, and he could just hear faint sounds from us. These were the times when his body was not functioning normally.

A couple of unique things about this day was that at the very same time of this encounter, my wife, Heather, was taking photos of the Toledo family, and there was supposed to be a special guest speaker at the children's

chapel, a missionary to Africa, but she was not able to
make the service for some reason.[1]

Conner's encounter was powerful and had dramatic lasting
affects on him. I was with his mother, Heather, at the time
because she was taking pictures of my kids. She received a phone
call letting her know that something dramatic was happening
with Conner—and that he had been taken from school deep in
an encounter with God. Ben explains it so well. This is something you pray for as a parent and absolutely want your children
to experience. Yet at the same time the package it sometimes
comes in can be uncomfortable and frightening.

I love how both Ben and Heather were able to stay in a
place of peace and encouragement while having the wisdom
to ask, "Is this God, and is this good?" Conner will never,
ever forget this experience. His heart was set on fire. I love the
ways of God—so unique, so unexplainable. I love that after
filling Conner with His power and light, He allowed him to
see deep into Africa and hear the joyful sounds of people
saying, "We're hungry no longer!" That prophetic promise
will be pivotal in Conner's life. I don't know why he needed
to see that. I don't know why God wanted him to hear that,
but God does. God knows. God knows what the future holds
for Conner. God knows what Conner needed deposited into
him in that moment. Only God. And God is infinitely faithful
and wise. He is unusual—His ways are not our ways. But how
glorious and how beautiful His ways are.

I have learned some things from watching God encounter
people. Sometimes the most profound encounters are simple,
quiet, and private. Sometimes He chooses to encounter

people in a dramatic and unexplainable way. It was like that all throughout the Bible. Stories of angelic visitations during which people shake and fall are not uncommon. Sometimes our mortal bodies cannot withstand God's powerful presence.

I don't know why God encounters some people one way and other people a different way. All I know is, I have grown to respect and appreciate every way God chooses to encounter mankind. What an honor. What a gift! The living God is passionate about pursuing us, encountering us, and revealing Himself to us. God was not just meant to be a concept we agree with intellectually. Since He created mankind in the garden, God always intended for us to truly know and experience Him. God loves to break into the natural realm with His power, His glory, and His love—and thank God that He does!

I pray that all of us will maintain a posture of peace and trust as we invite God's power and love into our lives. Even though His Spirit may lead us on an unknown journey, we will be forever marked and transformed.

> Blessed are the pure in heart, for they will see God.
> —Matthew 5:8

> At that time Jesus said, "I praise you, Father, Lord of heaven and earth, because you have hidden these things from the wise and learned, and revealed them to little children."
> —Matthew 11:25

> Your sons and your daughters shall prophesy...your young men shall see visions.
> —Joel 2:28, nkjv

Conner is happy and healthy today. His parents still don't fully understand why God encountered him in such a dramatic way, but they are glad they gave God room to move in their son's life, even though the experience was frightening and uncomfortable.

PART THREE

PRAYERS THAT CHANGE HISTORY

From the lips of children and infants you have ordained praise because of your enemies, to silence the foe and the avenger.

—Psalm 8:2

The person who trusts me will not only do what I'm doing but even greater things, because I, on my way to the Father, am giving you the same work to do that I've been doing. You can count on it. From now on, whatever you request along the lines of who I am and what I am doing, I'll do it. That's how the Father will be seen for who he is in the Son. I mean it. Whatever you request in this way, I'll do.

—John 14:12–14, The Message

PRAYERS THAT SHIFT LAWS

N 2002 CHILDREN in Kenya were becoming very empowered as saints in the kingdom. They began to realize they had a voice in the heavens and that they truly were seated with Christ. I began to hear so many reports about groups of children who were gathering to fast, pray, and seek God together. This was happening primarily in western Kenya, but it started spreading to other regions as children caught the vision.

These children were seeking God for their families, their schools, their communities, and their nation. I attended some of these prayer meetings, and typically there were groups of children crowded into a room, usually all piled on top of one another. One of the older kids would lead them in singing some songs. They would all sing loud and joyfully together. Then they would pray. Their prayers were beautiful—simple, humble, heartfelt, and powerful. I remember thinking, "If I were God, I would never be able to resist these prayers." They were just so pure.

Back in 2002 one of the major issues affecting the welfare of children in Kenya was the reality that free education did not exist. In fact, free primary education had not been available since the 1980s, and masses of children roamed the streets with no hope of education. Children in poorer communities were most affected, and since parents had to work all day, many of the nation's children were being left unattended and unprotected.

Not only were these children not being given much hope for a promising future, but also the fact that children were not in school during the day made them extremely vulnerable. Children were commonly victims of abuse, neglect, and exploitation. At this time Kenyan president Daniel Arap Moi had been in office since 1978 and seemed to be holding a tight rein on the nation's leadership. With the same government in office for twenty-four years, things certainly felt unmovable—at least to some people.

When President Moi began leading the country in 1978, he initially showed a lot of concern for issues affecting children. Because of the rise in violence and corruption across the nation, the economy had taken a hit, and many national programs had been cut. The children decided to focus their prayers around this issue. They were convinced that God had a great plan for the children in Kenya and that it was unjust for them to not all have access to education.

They began to pray fervently. Children across the nation pressed in through prayer and declared a shift in the laws hindering what God desired for the children in that nation. During these times of prayer and fasting the children called forth a shift in the laws and a release of what God wanted to do through children in Kenya.

With an election at hand, the children focused much of their prayers on a peaceful, violent-free transition of power. Within a few months there was a complete and peaceful government change, and a new president, Mwai Kibaki, took office on December 30, 2002. In less than a week he implemented a new universal primary education policy, which granted all children access to free education throughout the country. This was a huge success, and children all over celebrated their victory.

Not only did the prayers of these children help to shift a law in their nation, but their prayers also affected the levels of violence in their communities. In Bungoma there was a notorious group of criminals called "Mojo Kwisha" (which means something along the lines of, "They hit the door once and it is finished"). This troublesome group was famous for ransacking entire villages. They would steal, rape, beat, and traumatize everyone they came in contact with.

While the children were praying for the laws in their nation to change, they knew they also needed to pray for the violence to end. They focused much of their prayer efforts toward this issue, and during this time of prayer and fasting, many of these criminals were arrested, killed by police, or brought to salvation! Children were soon in school, and their communities were peaceful once again. It is truly as Psalm 2:8 says, "Ask of me, and I will make the nations your inheritance, the ends of the earth your possession."

ONE MILLION ANGELS

N December 2001, while I was living in Kenya, I became extremely ill with an "undiagnosed tropical disease." I was hospitalized and, because of the severity of my condition, was not given much hope of surviving. It all happened so quickly; suddenly I was dying all alone in a hospital in Africa at Christmastime.

My family had just found out I was sick and was scrambling trying to figure out how to get to me. I had been able to stay fairly positive, but as I lay there in my hospital room, I heard Christmas carolers passing through the hospital. Hearing them sing brought back all the warm and tender memories I had of Christmas with my family. Suddenly, for the first time since the whole ordeal began, I started to cry.

I pulled the thin bedsheet up over my face and just cried in the silence of my room. I whispered a prayer through my tears, "God, I feel so alone. I wish there was at least one person here with me right now, just one person who knows me and loves me." I felt so overwhelmingly alone. I drifted off to sleep in the solitude under the sheet.

I don't know if you've ever had a dream that is so real you seriously can't decide whether it actually happened or not, but that is what I experienced that day. I'm still not entirely sure whether it actually happened or if it was a dream. Either way, it changed me. The first thing that happened was I could see a gentleman sitting in the waiting room of the hospital just outside my door right by the nurses' station. He was dressed in a military uniform, and somehow I just knew he was a high-ranking official. He was sitting most of the time, but occasionally he would pace back and forth.

He seemed very invested in something. He was constantly checking with the nurses. When he realized I could see him, he winked at me and sweetly said, "I'm going to make sure you get out of here just fine, kid." Hope flooded into my heart. Who was this guy? Was I awake? Was I dreaming? Was he an angel?

All of a sudden I heard the Lord say, "Get up and look out the window." Miraculously able to move off my bed (I was hooked to multiple tubes/machines), I stood up and walked over to the little window just to the left of my bed. As I stood there, I was shocked by what I saw. The entire parking lot and beyond was full of soldiers standing at attention in perfect formation. It looked like one million soldiers!

Suddenly reality rushed into my thoughts. Why were there a million soldiers surrounding the hospital? What was going on? All of a sudden, as clear as could be, I heard the Lord speak to me. He said, "You are not alone! You have no idea how many angels I have dispatched to stand at attention on your behalf."

I was completely overwhelmed by the goodness of God toward me! I began to weep with such gratitude. All of a sudden the scene shifted, and I was being discharged from the hospital. The general from the waiting room had a bouquet of flowers for me in his right arm, and I was clinging to his left arm as he slowly walked me down the corridor, around a corner, down a flight of stairs, through another hallway, and eventually through some double doors that led right into the parking lot I had seen from my window. As soon as we stepped out, the sun blinded me momentarily. Then all I could see were military hats flying as a million soldiers cheered and whistled.

This experience made me feel absolutely, insanely loved and adored by my Father in heaven. In what was probably the loneliest moment in my life, God had sent one million angels to stand at attention on my behalf! Well, the story just gets better. I didn't come to find out this part of the story until months later when a woman I know came up to me after I returned home to California. She told me, "I've been dying to ask you something! Where were you, or what was going on with you three days before Christmas?" Before I could answer, she excitedly told me this story.

"Well, three days before Christmas, just before five in the morning, our daughter Tabitha (who is five years old) came running into our room rather alarmed and woke us up. When we asked her what was going on, she insisted that we needed to get up right then and immediately pray for you. We said, 'OK, Tabitha, let's pray.' She argued that we must get out of bed and get on our knees with her beside the bed. Thinking it rather odd, but definitely seeing how serious and intense she was about this, we pulled ourselves out of bed and joined her on our knees. With such passion she began to pray, 'Dear Jesus. You know exactly what Jennifer needs. Will You please send her one million angels right now? Thank You, Jesus.'"

As soon as she was done praying, she had a look of relief on her face and headed back to bed. Her parents thought it was so wild. She had never done anything like that before, and they had been dying to find out what was going on with me that day.

I seriously cannot even handle God sometimes. He absolutely blows my mind! God woke up a five-year-old girl in California and asked her to pray that He would send me one million angels in Nairobi, Kenya. She heard the invitation, she obeyed, and her prayers literally made the way for one million angels to be dispatched to Africa.

Not only that, but when she prayed at five in the morning, it was three in the afternoon in Kenya—shortly before the Christmas carolers came through the hospital. God had already provided the provision before I even knew I needed it. By the time I was having my little meltdown under my sheet, the provision I needed had already been dispatched from heaven.

I can't help but wonder why God chose to use this particular little girl across the world instead of someone else. The reality is, when I got sick, a fellow minister sent out a message all over the world, calling people to pray for me. There were many leaders, so-called "heavy hitters in the spirit," praying for me. Yet God chose to use a child to partner with Him for my miracle. I don't fully understand God's ways, but what I do know is that I love them.

I'll have to write another book and tell the whole story of how God healed me, because it's amazing! But for now, you'll have to be content with knowing that the day after this experience Jesus came into my hospital room and performed surgery on me, and I was instantly and totally healed! It was the most dramatic miracle I have ever personally experienced. The doctors were shocked, and there was no medical explanation for what happened.

When I was being discharged from the hospital, a dear Kenyan pastor named Simon, a man who had been like a father to me, showed up at the hospital to bring me flowers and drive me home. I was finally up out of my hospital bed. I had put on my own clothes and had just slipped on my shoes when I looked up to see Simon. I felt so very comforted by his presence. He grabbed my arm in his arm, as I was still very weak and needed to regain my strength from what my body had been through. I clung to his arm as he helped me walk slowly out of my room, down the hallway, around a corner, down a flight of stairs, and eventually through double doors that led me straight out to the parking lot.

It wasn't until that moment that everything registered. It was just like my experience. I was clinging to Simon's left arm, he had a bouquet of flowers for me in his right arm, and he had just walked me out of the hospital through a random back door exactly as the general had in my supernatural experience. As Simon opened the double doors, I was blinded by the beautiful sunlight I had not seen in several days. Instantly I knew that one million angels were celebrating! I couldn't help but be overwhelmed with emotion and gratitude. He had done it! It was just as Psalm 91:11 promises: God commanded His angels concerning me to guard me in all my ways.

10
WHEN PRAYERS SHAKE DARKNESS

A T ONE TIME in Kenya there was a lot of prayer targeting an uprising of witchcraft in the local communities. Children would gather each week and have intense times of intercession during which they would pray specifically that God would destroy the power of witchcraft, sorcery, and divination in the community. We later discovered that these prayers were really bothersome to a local sorcerer, and he intended to make sure they stopped. He insisted that the children's prayers had caused the snake he used for sorcery to die, and he wanted revenge.

At the same time Patrick, the pastor from Bungoma who spearheaded the children's movement I mentioned in chapter 1, was planning a large camp for children in cooperation with some other children's workers. They were expecting eight hundred children and one hundred adults to attend. On the very first day of the camp, the team prepared a big morning feast for all the children, and they were planning to serve them all traditional chai, which is a strong black tea that is mixed with milk and sugar.

Because children's ministers were hosting such a large event and children were coming from all over the region, they asked various members of the community to consider donating food for the event. The sorcerer whose snake died heard about the upcoming event and saw it as an opportunity to "punish" those who had been making his work so difficult. He disguised himself as a religious person and donated ten liters of milk, which he sent to the camp through another person.

Unbeknownst to us, the sorcerer had combined venom from his now dead snake with other poisons and mixed it into the milk. It was enough poison to kill the masses. The milk was delivered to the church, where the team was preparing for the children's arrival. Several of the Sunday school teachers had spent the night at the church so they could get up early to help make all the food for the morning feast.

As the chai was being prepared, God, in His unwavering love and faithfulness, spoke to the hearts of two of the leaders and told them the milk was unsafe and should be dumped out. The team dumped all the donated milk they had (even the good milk) and decided to simply make black tea for everyone. Someone had enough change to purchase three small packets of milk, but that was only enough to make chai for twenty to thirty people. So they decided to serve the chai to some of the distinguished guests and have everyone else drink tea without milk.

The chai (with milk) filled three medium-sized kettles, and the children serving the tea were instructed to serve the distinguished guests first. By this time the children had arrived for the camp and were gathered in the hall praising and worshiping God. Miracles began to happen. First, before serving the tea, the children prayed blessings over it. Before any of the leaders realized what had taken place, the children had served more than 150 cups of chai with milk, and the three kettles were just as full as when they started!

After the leaders realized what was happening, they allowed the children to continue serving the tea, and to everyone's amazement the quantity in those three kettles never changed! All eight hundred children were joyfully drinking tea with milk, as were an additional one hundred adults! That was the first of many miracles that day. The food multiplied as well, and everyone feasted. Many people were saved, and many received physical healing. One girl was totally healed of epilepsy during the children's meeting that day.

Later that day Patrick felt the Lord tell him to look at the area where the milk had been dumped out. It had been somewhere between seven and nine hours since the milk had been discarded there. A foul smell was coming from the area where the milk had been dumped because the insects and rats that tasted the milk had died instantly. A dog that licked the milk also lay dead.

Patrick remembers walking back into the room full of eight hundred beautiful children passionately singing and praising, and thinking that without God's divine intervention they all could have died. But instead, God would not allow the weapon formed against them to prosper (Isa. 54:17). The man who poisoned the milk waited to hear the story of mass deaths and was furious to hear that there were salvations, miracles, and healings instead.

Finally, on the third day of the event, the sorcerer came to the camp where the children were meeting and asked the staff if the milk he donated ever got used. Patrick told him the milk was "so sweet and that God multiplied it to be enough for more than nine hundred people." They went on to tell him about the many miracles that were taking place. Engulfed in rage, the man quickly stood up and ran away![1]

PART FOUR

RELEASING CHILDREN TO A BROKEN WORLD

*We are therefore Christ's ambassadors, as though
God were making his appeal through us. We implore
you on Christ's behalf: Be reconciled to God.*
—2 Corinthians 5:20

FINDING BARB

J ESSE WAS A sweet and hyper seven-year-old boy who loved to take risks. Sometimes his risk taking got him into trouble. But when he channeled his passion toward God, awesome things always happened! I loved taking Jesse out on outreaches because he just knew no fear. One particular morning I was helping a group of children prepare for an outreach we were going to lead later that day. I had them all find a quiet spot somewhere in the room and spend some time praying and asking God about the people He would be leading them to later in the day.

As God would show them things, the children would draw pictures or write words of encouragement to hand out as they encountered the people God had spoken to them about. Jesse sat curled up on the floor, intensely trying to focus on what God was saying. All of a sudden he sat up straight, grabbed some crayons, and went to work making a card. After a while, as I was making my rounds throughout the room, checking in on everyone, I passed by Jesse and saw a beautiful card that said "For Barb" on the front.

I asked him about the card, and he told me God told him he would meet a woman named Barb who would have brown hair, and that God had a special message for her. I opened up the card, and sweetly written inside were the words, "Barb,

God has not forgotten about you. You are the star of His eye." Jesse had lovingly decorated the card and filled it with stars. I loved it! I proceeded to ask Jesse if he had prayed about where Barb would be (which group he was to be in that day), and he quickly and cheerfully gave me a, "Yep! She'll be at Walmart."

"Perfect!" I said. Later that day Jesse got in the van that was heading to Walmart. We had allotted one hour for the children to walk around their outreach locations and love on people, hand out their cards and pictures, and see what God would do. Jesse wasn't about to waste any time. With his card in hand, he started going down every single aisle in Walmart asking every brunette if her name was Barb. I mean, that is some serious dedication right there! After about fifteen to twenty minutes of scouring Walmart, Jesse walks up to a woman, asks her if her name is Barb, and she says, "Yes! I'm Barb."

The look of absolute delight and accomplishment flooded Jesse's face, and he told her, "Great! I've been looking for you, because I have a card for you from God." Barb wasn't sure what to think, but she reached out and took hold of the card Jesse was excitedly handing to her. She read the front, "For Barb." Then she opened it up. Her eyes read over the words, and instantly tears began to run down her cheeks. Jesse began to share with her that God told him he would find her there today and that God really wanted her to know that He sees her and knows her and loves her and that she is the star of His eye.

The woman just wept right there in the middle of the aisle in Walmart. She held the card close to her heart and shared with Jesse how absolutely thankful she was for the card and for him. She told Jesse that someone she loved had just died, and she had been wondering if God really knew what she was going through or that she even existed. She was so undone by God's love for her and extravagance in finding her. She could not believe this little boy had been used by God to find her and put to rest this enormous struggle within her. Barb encountered Jesus through Jesse that day in Walmart, and she would never be the same.

THE CHILDREN OF COLIMA

I HAD THE PRIVILEGE of ministering to an incredible group of children in Colima, Mexico. These children were on fire for God and had such a passion to share their faith. After several days of ministry and training, we had planned to end the week by taking the children out to the streets of the city to evangelize and pray for their community. The kids were so excited and could hardly wait! Their leaders had helped the children pray and seek God about the particular neighborhood we were supposed to focus on—and the kids were just chomping at the bit to get out and love on people. We broke the children into small groups of four or five (we had about sixty children all together). And the children ranged in age from four to twelve.

We sent out one adult with each group of children but clearly explained to the adult that they were just there to look after the kids and encourage them, not to take over or "lead the way." We really wanted the kids to stretch themselves and take leadership in this. We had a several-block radius to cover and decided to meet back in four hours.

Each team was given a particular area to cover, but what they did within that area was entirely up to them. We encouraged them all to pray, get a strategy from God, and just do whatever He said. Some of them went from home to home, asking if there were any prayer needs. Some of them just prayer-walked around the neighborhood. Some of them picked flowers and handed them out to people on the street, speaking a word of encouragement as they did. We didn't want to give them a model. We wanted to give them tools to partner with God and the faith to obey!

Some of the children would stand outside a home and ask God some questions before walking up to the door: "God, what do You want to say to this family?" "What are You doing with this family?" "How can we serve this family?" Then when they would knock on the door, they were already bursting with God's heart for whoever would answer.

Incredible things would happen. The children would say things as simple as, "God wants you to know that He is your provider and knows what you need, and He sent us to tell you that you are His daughter and that He is going to take care of you." At house after house people were overwhelmed by God's heart for them and would get saved. Many people were healed as well!

The children would say, "God told us that He wants to heal someone's back here. Is there anybody who needs a healing in their back?" Sure enough, the person with the back injury would get healed (or whatever particular ailment God had shown the children). It was awesome! I kept thinking to myself, "I don't know anybody who likes going door-to-door to minister. These kids are loving it, and so many miracles are happening!"

It was great because there is just something so disarming about children. Many people thought they were coming to sell cookies or something of that nature. They were so nonthreatening—and so stinking cute! They always got invited in for cookies, and the kids thought this was the best day ever! Over shared cookies and milk, entire families would get saved!

In my particular group I was amazed by the boldness the children had. In fact, in all honesty, there were many moments in which the children's boldness left me feeling rather uncomfortable. Several times when the door opened, the first thing out of the child's mouth was, "Can I ask you a question? If you were to die today, do you know if you'd go to heaven or hell?"

I clearly was not the only one feeling a little uncomfortable, as the person standing there would start to squirm and wrestle through the question just presented to them. If the answer was, "I'm not sure," or something of that nature, the children would just lovingly share how they could be sure, and time after time they would lead people to Jesus.

I was amazed! These children could never in a million years win an argument about theology. Many of them didn't even know how to read the Bible. But they had such purity and faith and presented Jesus in an irresistible way! I was floored as house after house people were praying to receive Christ and encountering the love of God for the first time.

A Family in Mourning

I was so tempted to "adjust" how the children were interacting with people. I wanted to "soften up" their approach a little—to have them connect a little relationally with people before they dropped the "Are you going to heaven or hell" bomb. Just as I was about to talk with my group, I felt such a conviction from the Lord about letting them just be themselves—even in their rawness. In fact, it was their rawness that was so provoking. An adult just walking up to someone and saying, "Do you know if you going to heaven or hell?" probably wouldn't be received very well. But the genuine simplicity and purity flowing out of the kids were simply irresistible.

One door we knocked on was especially unique. I could hear many voices inside and the sounds of crying. I wasn't quite sure what we were stepping into, but it all quickly unfolded. Someone opened the door and explained to us that the family's son had just died, and the whole family had gathered to mourn. The kids shared with the mother that we were walking around the neighborhood praying for people and that we'd love to pray for them. As the mother warmly received us and invited us in, I started having a mini inner panic attack. I had no idea what would come out of these kids' mouths, and I had no time to give them the little "OK, people are really hurting right now; let's make sure we're super-sensitive to what they're going through" speech.

Desperately praying under my breath that we wouldn't offend this family, I gathered with the children and all the family members in the living room. Everyone in the family looked up at us through tear-stained faces; the grief was so heavy in the room. Before I could say anything, one of the kids, with such a look of sadness for this family, blurted out, "I'm so sorry your son is dead. That is so very sad. Did he know Jesus? Do you know if he is in heaven right now?"

Of course, awkward silence filled the room, and I wanted to disappear and pretend this wasn't happening. The awkward silence lasted for an inordinately long period of time, making it extra awkward. You could tell from the looks on the family's faces that they had not even thought about that. One by one the kids started to share about the love of God for this family and how life is just so short and that we are all invited to share in God's free gift of eternal life.

It was powerful. The family just sat there drinking in every word the kids were saying. One of the kids said, "All of us will end up dead one day. God sent us to you today so that you can know that death doesn't have to be the end. If you want to give your life to Jesus, get on your knees right now." Sure enough, all eleven family members, including the Catholic priest who was there, all got on their knees and prayed a prayer to receive Christ as their Lord and Savior.

It was so beautiful. The atmosphere in that home dramatically shifted, and life and hope could instantly be felt. We spent some time loving on that family, and they begged us to come back soon. We proceeded down the street we were on, and God continued to do such profound things with everyone we met.

As we were nearing the end of our time, I heard loud sirens quickly approaching us. I turned around to see a police car pull up right where we were. As the officer quickly jumped out, it was clear he was heading toward us. Confused about why this officer was stopping us, I stepped forward to speak with him. He came right up to us and said, "Are you the group of kids that has been going around this neighborhood talking to people and praying for people?" "Yeesss," I nervously responded. Thoughts started to race through my mind about how I was in Mexico, there was no other adult with me, my Spanish was decent but not amazing, and somehow it looked like we were in trouble with the law.

"Oh, thank God!" he responded. "I've been looking all over for you guys! I've had several families tell me that you guys talked to them and they got healed or they got right with God. I had to find you because I want to give my life to Jesus."

Right then this police officer got down on his knees on the sidewalk, and we were able to lead him to Jesus! It was awesome! He prayed with such sincerity and passion while kneeling on that sidewalk. He had heard that God was with us, and after he got right with the Lord, he wanted the children to pray for him. We had an incredible time ministering to that officer, and he left that day glowing.

At the end of the afternoon all of the groups gathered back together to share their stories about what God had done. Each group had amazing testimonies, and the kids were exploding with energy and joy! Each group submitted their tallies, and within four hours those 60 children had led 378 people to Jesus!

Three hundred seventy-eight people, including a Catholic priest and a police officer, were saved in one afternoon as children went door-to-door with simplicity, faith, and love. What a gift children are to us!

13
SAVED BY SMILEY FACES

RIANNA WAS FIVE years old and the cutest little blonde-haired, blue-eyed girl you had ever seen. She had come along on one of the outreaches we were leading with children in the downtown area of her city. Some of the older children had made prophetic cards and were handing them out to people, or they were just walking around talking to people and praying for them.

We encouraged the younger children like Arianna, who didn't know how to write, to just sit and people-watch and ask God to "highlight" someone to them. When they felt like God was bringing someone to their attention, they should ask God, "If You could draw this person any picture right now, what would You draw them?" When they got the picture, they would take crayons and blank paper and draw what they saw.

Arianna felt like God had highlighted a particular woman who was walking around shopping, and she felt God wanted to draw her a picture of smiley faces. Arianna filled her page with smiley faces—big smiley faces, small ones, purple ones, red ones, yellow ones, and so on. After Arianna drew her picture, we encouraged her to pray and ask God why He wanted to give this woman a picture of smiley faces. After a few moments of sitting there with her eyes closed, she exclaimed that she had the answer and asked if one of our team members would help her take it to the woman.

Arianna and one of our team members walked over to where the woman was. Arianna handed her the drawing and said, "Hi! This is a picture for you. It's from God." The woman was definitely caught by surprise and saw the very simple smiley faces and smiled kindly at the little girl. She said thank you and was about to keep walking when Arianna said, "Do you know why God wants to give you a picture of smiley faces?"

The woman, rather intrigued at this point, said, "No, do you?" Arianna said very matter-of-factly, "God wants you to know that when He sees you, He's not mad at you! He smiles!" The woman burst into tears right on the spot. Obviously there was much more going on. She proceeded to tell Arianna and the female team member who was with her that she used to be a follower of Jesus but had walked away from Him and made many bad choices. As she sobbed, she said, "I can't believe this is happening! Just right now I was walking down the street having an argument with God in my head. I kept telling Him, 'I know You must be so mad at me. I know You could never forgive me.' And then right here this little girl stops me and interrupts my inner argument to hand me this picture of smiley faces and to tell me that God is not mad at me!"

Our team got to love on and minister to that precious woman that day. She recommitted her life to the Lord and stepped into grace and His love over her. She could have lived her whole life wrestling with shame and feeling like God would never be pleased with her. In a moment—in one moment—a little five-year-old girl connected with God's heart and was used by heaven to help rescue her out of her prison. The woman was saved by smiley faces from the lies that were destroying her. God is so beautiful!

14
ORANGE AND BANANA

THREE YOUNG BOYS aged four, six, and eight were put together when we divided children into groups to head off on a big adventure with the Holy Spirit in a large mall. We told them there were no rules; they just needed to listen to the Holy Spirit and do whatever He told them to do. Their only objective was to love people.

The teams of children started to disperse throughout the mall, and this particular group of boys lingered by the entrance, praying and asking God for some clues about what they should do. (Now, for those of you moms reading this, we didn't send children out alone. There was an adult assigned to each group of kids whose job was to intercede and be there to help if the kids needed them.) Anyway, as these three little guys prayed, they asked God to give them some kind of sign about where they should go. All of a sudden the little four-year-old burst out with, "I saw an orange and a banana!"

The other two boys weren't quite sure what that was supposed to mean or how to interpret it, but the four-year-old was so confident about what he saw. So they asked God what orange and banana meant. All of a sudden one of the boys got the idea, "I think we're supposed to go to Orange Julius [the smoothie shop]." Excited about their discovery, they began to head over to Orange Julius in the mall. As they approached the place, they realized that there were no customers in there, just one woman behind the counter.

The boys decided that God must have sent them for her, so they stood back and began to ask God some questions about her. One of the boys suddenly felt overwhelmingly sad and told his friends, "I think she's sad about something." They asked God to show them what was making her so sad, and one of the boys felt like someone in her family had just died. They were a little nervous about striking up a conversation in case they hadn't heard right, but they decided they had nothing to lose.

They approached the counter and nudged one another, hesitant about who was going to talk first. Finally the oldest boy said, "Excuse me, can we ask you a question?"

"Sure!" the woman replied.

"Well, you can tell us if we're wrong, but we were praying for you, and we felt like you might be really sad. Are you feeling sad?"

The woman couldn't hold back her tears. She stood there and nodded her head that she was sad as tears just ran down her cheeks. They proceeded to ask more. "Did someone in your family recently die?" The woman looked shocked as these three little boys were cluing into something so deep and tender in her life. She eventually was able to pull herself together and shared how her mother and sister had recently been killed in a car accident, and this was her first day back to work.

Those three little boys got to shower that sweet woman with so much love and prayer that day. They told her the whole story about "orange and banana" and how God led them to her. They told her He did that because He wanted her to know He understood her pain and was with her. She was so amazingly blessed and had a true encounter with the love of God that day! She was stunned that God would send three young boys to her workplace, on her first day back, just to tell her that He was with her and loved her. How could she not fall in love with such an amazing God?

"GOD LOVES YOU AND YOUR TATTOOS!"

W E WERE IN Shreveport, Louisiana, and had just finished an equipping session with a great group of children. Kids were sprawled all over the floor with paper and crayons making prophetic cards to be handed out later in the day. I couldn't help but notice that one little boy's card said, "God loves you and your tattoos!" in huge letters across the front.

Very curious, I asked him some questions about his card. He proceeded to tell me that this card was for a guy he saw who had blue jeans, a black shirt, a black-and-white bandana, and tattoos. It sounded as though he was describing someone he knew, so I asked him if he knew the guy, and he said, "No, I just saw him." Assuming he meant he "saw" him at the conference we were attending, I said, "Oh, you mean you saw him here at the conference?"

The boy looked at me like, "Wow, this chick is slow," and said, "No! I saw him in the Spirit."

"Ooohhh! Got it!" I said. "Awesome!" I encouraged him to ask God for more details about what He wanted to say to this man and which outreach location he was to visit in order to find this person. The boy informed me that he had already asked those questions and the man would be at the grocery store.

Well, later that day, that little boy headed out with the group of kids invading the big grocery store with love. He looked everywhere for the man he "saw" while he was praying. He searched and searched but could not find him anywhere. He was growing discouraged, as their time was coming to an end and they needed to head back to the bus.

He started to question whether he had heard correctly and just decided he would hand it to a random guy in the produce section. He walked up to the man and asked, "Do you by chance have tattoos?" The man looked clearly irritated by the disruption and said, "No," rather abruptly. The boy felt so defeated but handed the card to the man and said, "Well, here's a card for you anyway."

The man said, "I don't want your card!" and walked away.

The poor kid was on the brink of tears. Not only had he "missed it," but now he felt majorly rejected. He dragged his feet through the parking lot heading back to the bus with the only card he never handed out. He was just so sure he had seen the one who was supposed to have that card.

Just as he was about to step onto the bus, guess who he saw across the parking lot. Yep, there he was. A man walking toward the store wearing blue jeans, a black shirt, a black-and-white bandana on his head, and covered in tattoos! The little boy was so excited. He raced over toward the man with a huge smile on his face. As he got close, he yelled out, "There you are! Where have you been? I've been looking all over for you!"

The guy looked pleasantly shocked by this introduction, and the little boy quickly handed him the card he had so lovingly made and told him God had asked him to make it for him. He continued to share with the guy all that God had put in his heart for him. He showered him with the love of the Father, and the man was evidently touched!

He was squatting down in the parking lot, eye to eye with this little boy, undone by the love of God! He got teary-eyed as he shared his story of feeling rejected in church because of his tattoos and how he felt like his tattoos had kept him from God. Those walls came down that moment in the parking lot, and he told the little boy he would keep his card forever. They exchanged a heartfelt hug, and both went on that afternoon with a glow that wasn't there before.

THE PERFECT TREASURE HUNT

W E WERE IN Red Deer, Alberta, Canada, and had dispersed teams of children all over the city. The kids were pumped and excited to see what God was going to do. One particular group of kids had spent some time before they left praying and writing down "clues" God was showing them about the "treasure" He was leading them to that day.

As they prayed, each child on the team contributed one thing he felt God was showing him. One child saw a "blue shirt," one saw "red hair," one saw "green eyes," one heard "park," and one little girl didn't see or hear anything but felt really strongly that she needed to make a card that explained how someone could find God. So she proceeded to write out a really great card explaining how someone could give his life to Jesus and what the gospel is all about.

The particular mom we assigned to that group was not from Red Deer and didn't know the area at all. We told her not to worry; God would lead them wherever they needed to go. The kids all loaded in the minivan, and they started their journey. The only directional clue they had was "park," so they decided to start by looking for a park.

The mom announced to the kids that she had no idea where a park was, so they would have to ask Holy Spirit which direction to go. The kids started yelling out, "Left!"; "Turn right here!"; "Second left!" She just followed their cues and, sure enough, they ended up at a park. Everyone was squealing with excitement that they had heard right.

At first glance it appeared that no one was in the park, but just before discouragement set in, they noticed one woman off in the distance sitting on a park bench. As they drove closer, the kids all started yelling, "She has red hair and a blue shirt!" Just as the mom parked, the kids jumped out of the van and ran full speed over to this woman. They were so excited to have found their treasure. Sure enough, the woman sitting in the park had a blue shirt, red hair, and green eyes.

I'm sure the woman felt confused about why an excited mob of children were running toward her. But as the kids rambled to her about her being their treasure and how God had sent them to her, she quickly warmed up. Just then the little girl remembered the card she had made. She pulled it out and handed it to the woman and said, "Here you go. This clearly is for you."

The woman sitting in the park opened the card and read every word that had been so thoughtfully written. It was like she was just drinking in truth. She started to cry, then laugh, then cry—all while telling the kids that she was so thankful that God had "found her." She shared with them that for the last few months she had been searching for God. She acknowledged that she didn't know how to find God and didn't really know much about Him, but she really wanted to know who He was.

She had been praying (just as she was doing in the park before the children arrived) the same prayer she had prayed so many times in those few months: "God, I don't know how to find You. Will You please find me?" She sat there in amazement, taking in the reality that God had found her. Every word on that card was written perfectly for her, and the kids got to lead her in accepting Christ as her personal Lord and Savior.

Not only did she get saved that day, but she also was healed of a knee injury and filled with the Holy Spirit! She had a dramatic and radical encounter with Jesus! That woman went into the park lost and alone and left not only knowing who Christ is but also having personally and powerfully experienced Him!

17
THE SHOE SHINER

AFTER TEACHING A large group of children in Kenya for a few days, I commissioned them to walk in the fullness of the kingdom and to carry the kingdom wherever they went. We had a really special and powerful time with the children during the meetings.

One evening after the seminar had ended, I was walking around town with a few of the wonderful street children I had come to know. We noticed a small crowd of about two hundred people, all gathered around someone on a corner. Not sure what was happening, but in company of like-hearted curiosity, we nudged our way into the crowd to see what everyone was doing. It was one of the most beautiful sights I had ever seen.

There in the middle of all of these people was the most passionate and tender little boy, who happened to be a local shoe shiner, standing on his shoe-shining box preaching his little heart out. He was speaking with such deep love and authority. I just stood there unable to move, taking it all in. People were captivated by his words and the "Jesus" who just dripped out of him.

Everyone just stood there listening, his words carried such weight. I leaned over and asked the boys with me, "Who is he?" They looked at me, shocked by the question. They said,

"He was one of the kids at the conference! You told us we should preach the gospel—so that's what he's doing."

There were hundreds of children at the conference. There was no way I could remember each one, but in that moment I never felt more proud of anybody. Here was this tiny boy— he didn't look any older than seven or eight. He was humble, uneducated, and most likely unwanted. But he stood there as tall and regal as a prince, and love flowed out of him.

He had heard that God wanted to use him, so walking home from church, he decided not to waste a moment and went right to it. He led the majority of that crowd to Jesus that day. He prayed for people's healing and deliverance. People were visibly moved and encountered Jesus that evening on that street corner.

I will never forget that moment as I watched that precious little shoe shiner give his all for Jesus on that corner. There were so many people whose lives were changed that night because of him, but I think my life was changed the most. I had the realization that something so genuine, so beautiful, so powerful, and so passionate is built into the DNA of this generation, and it's just waiting to be given permission to shine. It's time for them to shine!

PART FIVE

HEALING HANDS

And these signs will accompany those who believe: In my name they will drive out demons; they will speak in new tongues; they will pick up snakes with their hands; and when they drink deadly poison, it will not hurt them at all; they will place their hands on sick people, and they will get well.

—Mark 16:17–18

MALARIA HEALED

A S YOU'VE READ in previous chapters, we have led multiple teams of children into the hospitals in Kenya. As different regions across Kenya caught word of how God was using children, they often would ask that a team come out and help train the children in their region. This kind of thing happened quite often.

After one of these regional trainings, we sent teams of children out all over the city. My husband, Jona, had the privilege of leading a small team of children to the local hospital. Their hearts were instantly broken over the large ward that was full of babies who had contracted malaria. There were between fifty and sixty babies in one room, and almost all of them were suffering from malaria. They were very sick, and the mothers there with them were all desperate for God to heal their children.

It was a really special time as the children ministered to each baby and mother. The kids could feel the Father's heart over each one so strongly, and their prayers were simple yet powerful. When Jona left with the group of children, they could really sense God moving in that infant ward. We asked the local pastor we were working with to please follow up with that hospital, particularly with that ward because we knew God was doing something there.

The next day the pastor phoned the hospital director to thank him for allowing us to visit and pray for patients. He asked him how everyone was doing. The director was so excited to give him the news that they had released almost all of the babies that morning—because the malaria was gone and the babies were all doing well! Praise God! Nearly sixty babies were healed of malaria and discharged from the hospital within twenty-four hours of receiving prayer. Our God is powerful!

19

WHEN A BABY RELEASES HEALING

LOVE THIS STORY for so many reasons. One reason is because it is about my daughter, Malaika. Another reason is because it just blows our paradigm when God uses an infant to release a miracle. It's so unexpected, so profound.

> Out of the mouth of babes and nursing infants You have ordained strength, because of Your enemies, that You may silence the enemy and the avenger.
> —PSALM 8:2, NKJV

We were ministering in Ecuador, and my husband and I were preparing to preach in a Sunday morning service. My husband is actually from Guatemala but spent most of his childhood in Ecuador, where his parents are missionaries and church planters. To this day my husband's immediate family all still live in Ecuador and work in the ministry there.

Because we had just arrived with our new daughter, who was about five months old at the time, I asked my sister-in-law to watch over her while we were ministering. I specifically asked her to please not pass her around; she was the only one to hold her. Being from the Latino culture, I knew that if she let one person hold her, then she'd have to let everyone hold her, and when I finally got her back, she would smell like thirty different old-lady perfumes and have dark red lipstick kisses all over her face.

My sister-in-law, Melania, was happy about that because as a new aunt who lived far away from her niece, she had no intentions to share her anyway. Shortly after this conversation, Melania was standing in the back of the church holding Malaika when a woman walked up to her. This woman and her husband had struggled with infertility for years, and everyone who knew this couple wanted to see them blessed with children. When the woman walked up to Melania, she immediately asked if she could hold the baby. Just as Melania was about to say no and give her little spiel as to why not, she suddenly felt the Lord urge her to hand Malaika to this woman.

Not understanding why she was doing it, Melania said, "Sure," and handed Malaika to her. All of a sudden while the woman was holding Malaika, she began to feel the presence of God sweep over her. She was deeply moved and said, "God is doing something!" Melania was feeling the presence of God strongly too and started prophesying over the woman. She told her, "God is healing you right now. Just as you grabbed Malaika—there is healing being released to you through her right now!"

They were both getting totally rocked by God. Now, for Melania to share this word with the woman was huge because she knew this poor woman had been prayed and prophesied over many times, and Melania did not want to set her up for disappointment. But something powerful took place when she handed Malaika over to her. God used a tiny baby girl who couldn't even talk to carry His presence and release heaven into a situation.

Sure enough, a few weeks later we received a phone call saying she was pregnant! After years of prayer and struggling, this woman finally received a breakthrough—and God decided to use a baby to release it. God never ceases to amaze me!

I've told Malaika, who is now six, this story many times, and she loves it. Since this time, whenever we are ministering and the Lord shows us that He wants to heal barrenness, I always have Malaika pray with me for the women because I believe she carries an anointing for healing. Together we have seen several women healed and receive their promise of a child. What a blessing!

In fact, one time while ministering in South Korea, I told Malaika to be ready because I was going to bring her out to help me pray for women who wanted to have children. She was three at the time. I found out later that in the child care room when her translator stepped out for a little while, Malaika had lined up all the little girls against the wall and was praying for them. The woman who was watching them just thought she was ministering to the girls and allowed her to carry on. When the translator came back into the room, she heard Malaika praying that God would put babies in all of their tummies so that they could be happy! They had a good laugh and sweetly explained to Malaika that these girls weren't old enough to be mommies yet. I, of course, thought it was awesome! That's my girl! Just practicing!

In all honesty, I think it's so great to teach your children how to pray and believe God for the supernatural. Sometimes at home one of us will pretend to be dead, and the others will have to pray for that person to be raised from the dead. My kids love this game! I know, to some of you that probably sounds super twisted and morbid. But it's fun, and the kids are practicing praying for life! Sometimes at the pool we practice walking on water. Sometimes we'll pray that God will turn our boring dinner into something amazing! Or we'll pray that we get transported on long road trips. We love to practice, and I want to create an environment in my home where the supernatural is just... natural.

HEALINGS IN EVERYDAY PLACES

M

Y HEART, WHEN training kids, is to just have them learn to stay connected to God at all times. There should not be areas of their lives that are "spiritual" and segments that aren't. They are in God, and He is in them—always. I encourage them to pay attention to what God is doing all the time, even in the boring, everyday places (like when their mom is dragging them around Target). We can turn everyday places into God adventures if we'll just keep our eyes and ears open.

I've had so many parents share wonderful stories with me about how in the middle of the grocery store their child told them that she really felt like she was supposed to pray for someone in the cereal aisle. They'll head over there and, sure enough, find someone there who needs healing or a touch from God—and powerful things end up happening. One mom told me that her shopping experience was much more pleasant when she decided to give her daughter blank paper and crayons. The daughter would curl up in the cart and draw pictures from Jesus for people they would pass in the store. That is awesome! Not only was this mom having a much more peaceful shopping experience, but in the midst of it people also were getting blessed and healed and even saved!

One time we took a team of kids down to Costco, and

while walking through the store, we would ask people if they needed healing for anything. Of course, we didn't want to disrespect the store or be insensitive to people's time, so we were very casual and relational. One woman had a brace on her leg and told us she was in a lot of pain and couldn't walk without the brace because she had injured her leg. The handful of kids gathered around her and prayed for God to release healing to her because He just loved her so much! It was a really sweet time, and she told us, "Wow! I'm not feeling any pain anymore! I think my leg is better!"

The kids were excited for her healing, but in times like these I have to be honest. Sometimes the thought runs through my head, "Is she really healed? Or is she just being nice and wanting to encourage the kids?" Either way, off we went, blessing her and looking for others who needed healing. Shortly after that, we saw her talking with someone and pointing toward us. It was obvious she was telling that person what happened and that they should come over to receive prayer. And the coolest thing was she had taken the brace off of her leg and was carrying it in her arms, walking totally fine without it! She thought she was coming to Costco for a roasted chicken, and she left with a healed leg! She smiled and waved the brace at us—telling us she felt amazing! Yay, God!

THE BODY PARTS ROOM IN HEAVEN

A FTER I SHARED with a group of children in California about their ability to access heaven, I had
them find a quiet spot in the room where they were
instructed to wait on God and ask Him to show them some
of the treasures in heaven. It was evident that several of the
children were having powerful experiences. After about twenty
minutes, I asked if any of the kids wanted to share with the
group what God had shown them.

Several shared really cool experiences and revelation God
had given them during their time. One little girl named
Kayla came up to me personally and whispered in my ear
that she saw something but didn't want to tell everyone (she
was extremely shy). She proceeded to tell me how she had
asked Jesus what He wanted to show her in heaven, and then
all of a sudden she was standing at a door. She opened the
door and was shocked by what she saw. The room was filled
with every kind of body part.

She explained how there were new arms, new legs, new
eyes, new hearts, and so forth. At first she thought it was
kind of gross and weird, but then God told her that heaven
lacks nothing and that if she ever knew anyone who needed
a new body part, she could just come up and get one! All
she needed was faith. She was amazed by the experience and

never expected to see something like that. I encouraged her and told her God is the ultimate creator, and He can always create a new body part for someone. I told her God showed her that because He wanted to put faith in her heart for that.

Kayla smiled sweetly and went back to her seat. About fifteen minutes after all of this, three people I had never seen before walked through the back doors of the room where I was meeting with the children and interrupted our session. I asked how I could help them, and the woman in the group said, "Can you please pray for this man? We heard that God was using the children here to heal people." We had been taking the kids out to the streets to pray for people all week, and apparently word of what we were doing had spread.

"Sure!" I said. It was evident the man needed healing, as he was being held up by his two friends. They helped bring him down to the front where we were, and all of the children gathered around him to pray. I asked what he needed prayer for, and he began to tell us about the severity of his condition. He had severe intestinal cancer and had been told there was nothing more the doctors could do. He needed a miracle (a new intestine), or he wouldn't live. Instantly I remembered Kayla's experience and looked over to see if she was going to step up. The kids all started laying hands on him and praying. Finally Kayla pushed through her shyness and stepped forward and placed her hand on the man and prayed a simple yet absolutely faith-filled prayer that God would release from the body parts room a new intestine for this man.

Instantly the man kind of jumped, looking very uncomfortable, and quickly mumbled a thank-you to the kids and walked quickly out of the building. His friends looked rather confused and unsure as to why he left so abruptly, and they followed him out. I had no idea what had happened. I wasn't sure if Kayla's prayer had offended him or freaked him out or what. But I was unable to go after him to find out because I couldn't leave the children alone. The whole thing was really random.

The next day as I was in the middle of a session with the children, the church secretary walked into the room and said there was a call for me, and with a smile on her face she said, "And you should take it." I picked up the phone, and, sure enough, it was the man from the day before. He was calling to apologize for running out so quickly. He told me, "When that little blonde girl prayed for me, something happened! I felt something! It felt like something jumped inside of me or something. It was bizarre, and it kind of freaked me out, because I had never experienced anything like that before. I got nervous and just left, but then on my way home I realized that I had no pain! I was in absolute shock because I always have terrible pain. By the time I was home I was hungry and wanted to eat something. Now, that is not possible. With my stage and type of cancer I cannot just 'eat,' but I did! I ate! 'That's impossible,' I kept thinking. I still didn't have any pain. I called my doctor right away, and he didn't believe me. He told me that without a new intestine I could not eat without excruciating pain. He insisted I come in and have a thorough evaluation. I wanted to call you personally and tell you that I'm convinced I have a brand-new intestine! I'm healed!"

THE NEWT

JIMMY WAS TURNING eleven years old, so his family decided to head up to Quail Lake to spend the weekend camping and celebrating his birthday. One afternoon a few of the guys decided to go out for a drive, and as they were driving along, they noticed a bright orange newt walking right down the middle of the road. Jimmy loved lizards and frogs, so they pulled the car over. Jimmy was ecstatic about his new find. He scooped up the newt and took him back to the campsite to show the others.

The particular amphibian was a fire newt. It was bright orange in color and had completely captured Jimmy's heart. He had absolutely fallen in love with this little creature. Right away Jimmy's mom, Sonja, knew there was something special about this newt and felt it was a gift from God for Jimmy, especially since they were celebrating his birthday. Jimmy held the newt with so much affection and named him "Fig" (short for Fig Newton, of course). After some deliberation, Sonja and her husband decided Jimmy could keep Fig as his pet.

When the family returned home from camping, Jimmy ran to put his new pet in a plastic aquarium he kept outside that had an assortment of tadpoles and frogs in it. The aquarium sat in the shade with a little water. Jimmy placed

Fig inside; then he and his dad headed off to Walmart to buy some supplies for the aquarium. While Jimmy and his dad were out running errands, the sun moved, exposing the little plastic aquarium to the full light of the sun. When Jimmy returned home, to his great dismay he found all of the creatures, including his new newt, stiff and lifeless. Jimmy quickly ran Fig inside, and Sonja's first response was, "No way! He's going to be fine. God is going to raise him back right now."

They held Fig under cold water for an hour hoping it would change things. But unfortunately his stiff, lifeless body did not change. Jimmy was devastated. He cried with such grief and guilt for having left his pet outside in the sun. Sonja was wrestling with Fig's death herself. It just didn't seem to make sense. She had no doubt in her mind that Fig was God's gift for Jimmy and that Fig was meant to live and not die. She had no doubt that God could raise him in that very moment. Yet Fig still wasn't moving. This just didn't seem to make sense. Sonja and Jimmy cried together, and as she held him, Sonja told Jimmy, "God is still God. God is powerful. If Fig is not being raised, it's not because of God's limitations. It's because of mine. There must be something in me that just isn't ready, that isn't lined up quite right yet."

Sonja tried hard to make sense of all that was happening. She felt such faith and could really sense that this was not supposed to happen. After crying together and spending some time praying, Sonja and Jimmy decided to bury Fig in the orchard behind their home. Jimmy made a little cross and put it on top of the little grave he and Sonja dug between the rows of trees.

Although he buried Fig, Jimmy continued to pray for a

miracle, but Sonja could see that he was losing hope. He was absolutely heartbroken and tormented with guilt over the death of his newt. On the second night after Fig had been buried, Jimmy was so distraught about the newt he went to bed shaking and had a terrible nightmare that somebody stepped on Fig's cross, and it pierced Fig in the heart. Upon waking Jimmy begged his parents, "Please! Please! We must dig him up and rebury him!" Seeing how very concerned he was, Sonja promised that she would rebury him the next day in a place that was safer. Sonja couldn't help but think about how gruesome of a task it would be to dig up the dead newt and frightened that she would chop it in half while trying to dig it up, but she knew Jimmy wouldn't be able to rest until it was done.

The next day while the kids were down the road playing, Sonja decided it was time for her to tackle this the dreaded feat. Equipped with rubber gloves, a container, and a shovel, Sonja walked out toward the orchard. It had been three days since Fig had died, and she too just could not find peace. "I knew that I knew it was God's will for Fig to live!" she said. And as she was walking toward Fig's grave, she changed her prayer. Instead of praying, "Please God, perform this miracle," she began to pray, "God, change me. Fix whatever needs to be fixed in me so that You can work through me."

While Sonja was still about one hundred yards away, she thought to herself, "If John (her Spirit-filled neighbor) were here with me, we could do this!" Then, as clear as could be, she heard the Lord say to her, "Hon, if you needed John, John would be here." The message was loud and clear: she didn't need a person to help her; she only needed God. Then all of a sudden she had a vision. From the corner of her left eye she saw the Lord suddenly appear and begin to walk beside her right in step with her. Sonja was filled with such hope and excitement! She confessed, "In all honesty, the extent of my faith was that He was going to help me to dig him up without cutting him in half. That's all I really had faith for in that moment."

When she arrived at the little cross in the orchard, she stood over it and prayed for a moment. Carefully positioning the shovel, she dug down into the earth and scooped up a big pile of dirt. There on the end of her shovel was the decomposing body of poor Fig. The smell of death filled her nose as she saw that his flesh had turned black and was rotting. He had been dead for three days. He was dry and shriveled up. His arms look like nothing more than threads, and his eyes were gone. He was flat, skeletal, and stiff as a board. Just as she was taking in the gruesome sight, Fig's lifeless body rolled off the shovel and fell back into the hole. Sonja, slightly nauseated by the whole thing, leaned over the hole and said, "Fig, live in the name of Jesus!" She told me later, "It was actually more of a beg than a prayer." She longed to partner with what was on God's heart for her son. What happened next took her breath away.

A MIRACLE IN THE ORCHARD

Sonja stepped back to take off her gloves, and out of the corner of her eye she saw one of Fig's little shriveled legs twitch. Shocked and unsure if her eyes were playing tricks on her, she quickly reached down, picked up his rotting body, and began to worship God. At this point both of his legs were twitching and moving. Sonja was in absolute awe that this was happening. Fig's little decomposing body was somehow starting to squirm in her hand, and she just wept and trembled and couldn't stop thanking God! He still had no eyes, his arms were dry, shriveled-up threads, and his body was rotten-looking and black—but he was moving!

Sonja saw the kids down the dirt road, and she started to scream for them to come. The kids came running, and when they were about thirty feet away from her, Jimmy just stopped dead in his tracks. Through her tears Sonja exclaimed, "Jesus raised Fig from the dead!" At this point, still looking and smelling like death, Fig had turned his body around in her hand and was no longer lying on his back. Jimmy was in utter amazement and carefully crept up to where his mother was standing. Unwilling to hold Fig, Jimmy just stayed close by and took it all in. Sonja looked into Jimmy's eyes and said, "Do you realize what Jesus did for you?" It was a powerful moment as a miracle took shape right before them.

They carried Fig back into the house and placed his frail body under running water. Little by little, the dead black skin covering his body began to flake off, and his color began to slowly return. Then he suddenly blinked, and his empty eye sockets all of a sudden had eyes. They were all so overwhelmed with this unbelievable miracle happening in their midst, Jimmy asked his mom, "What should we do?" She told him, "Well, you need to clean out the aquarium." By this time some of the neighbors had heard what was happening and had come over to witness the miracle. The kids had pulled out their cameras and captured the amazing miracle on film. The whole process took about five hours. All of Fig's "dead" skin shed off his body, and it regained its normal shape and color, except for one small spot on his back that stayed black. It was unbelievable. Fig was alive!!

For the next two weeks Fig lived with Jimmy and his family. He looked healthy but for some reason was refusing to eat. Unsure if Fig was sad or if he was sick, they continued to love and cherish their pet. Mother's Day was exactly two weeks later, and they decided to take Fig to church with them to share the resurrection testimony with their congregation. Just as they thought, their church marveled as Jimmy and Sonja shared the miraculous story and showed pictures of everything that had taken place—including photos of a very dead Fig. Faith electrified the room, and Fig was passed around from family to family. So many church members gained a new faith for healing and resurrections! This is so special to me personally, because I know many of the families in this church and was excited that they were able to witness such a powerful testimony. I have had the privilege of ministering in this church several times, and I happened to be speaking there shortly after that Mother's Day service and heard Sonja retell the testimony. The Father's love for Jimmy was so apparent throughout the whole story; I could just see God's hand woven throughout every detail.

After sharing the testimony at their church on Mother's Day, the family spent some time talking and praying about what should happen to the newt. Finally the family decided that Fig should be returned to his home at Quail Lake. God had so used Fig to awaken new levels of faith in this family and to show them how great their Father's love is for them. It was time for Fig to go home where he could thrive. After church the family drove up to the same area where they found Fig weeks earlier. Jimmy got out and searched all over to find the very best spot to release Fig. On the bank of the creek sat a perfect rock, so after heartfelt good-byes, Jimmy's family stood back and let Jimmy place Fig on the rock.

Fig sat there for a moment and then jumped into the water. Immediately he started swimming ecstatically in circles as if he knew he was home. After fifteen to twenty victory laps, he swam back to where Jimmy was crouched down on the bank, climbed up on the rock, and turned himself to look right into Jimmy's eyes. He stayed there for a moment, as if he and Jimmy were having a silent, heartfelt conversation. As Fig continued to peer into Jimmy's eyes, Jimmy smiled sweetly at him and said, "You're welcome, Fig." As soon as he did, Fig turned around, jumped back into the water, and swam away.

Jimmy's parents stood a few feet behind him and wept. Fig had been such a gift from God for Jimmy, and it had done so much to build the whole family's faith. When I spoke with her recently, Sonja said Jimmy now has no doubt that God loves him. He is completely confident in the fact that every day is a gift from the Father. He and the rest of the family are able to rest in the knowledge that life and death are in the hands of God. Fig's death brought so much guilt and pain and regret into Jimmy's heart. But the intimate way that God worked out every detail, even the sweet part of Fig lovingly saying good-bye to Jimmy, changed everything for Jimmy. Now instead of regret Jimmy sees that God had a bigger plan in Fig's death and that God's power is greater than even the most insurmountable obstacle.

ESTHER—THE MIRACLE WORKER

STHER WAS AN eleven-year-old Kenyan girl who loved Jesus very much. She had been attending classes at her church, which trained children in the work of the kingdom. One Saturday morning she traveled to her aunt's home to visit her for the day. When she arrived, she discovered her aunt's young child was extremely ill, and they were just preparing to take the child to the hospital. Just as they were getting ready to leave for the hospital, the child started to convulse violently and then dropped lifelessly to the ground. Everyone started to panic and cry, and the young child just lay lifelessly on the ground.

The Sunday before this happened, Esther's pastor taught on the steps to praying for healing. Esther knew there was no time to spare, so she boldly jumped up and grabbed the child. She later recounted that because the child was dying, she couldn't properly go through all the steps, so she took a "shortcut." She knew God was with her, and she just bound up the spirit of death. Immediately the child started breathing normally and began to act as if nothing ever happened.

Esther suddenly realized that a crowd had gathered, and all eyes were staring not at the healed child but at her, the miracle worker. When Esther tried to return the child, her aunt refused to take the child and insisted that only Esther hold the child. The aunt proceeded to beg young Esther to please stay one more day. Everyone knew Esther had the faith and the authority to bind up sickness and death and release life. In their hearts she was treasured as the miracle worker.

Esther went home the following week, and on Sunday she shared the powerful testimony at her church. Her pastor said Esther's testimony became the sermon that day, and many adults in the congregation were inspired and provoked by her ability to push past what she saw in the natural realm and press in to the heart of God for the situation.

PART SIX

A CHILD SHALL LEAD THEM:
THE ROLE OF CHILDREN IN GLOBAL REVIVAL

Then he said to his disciples, "The harvest is plentiful but the workers are few. Ask the Lord of the harvest, therefore, to send out workers into his harvest field."

—MATTHEW 9:37–38

THE DIVINE SETUP

A CCORDING TO THE latest statistics available to us today, there are an estimated 7 billion people living on the planet. The human population has skyrocketed in the last century to the point that there are more people on the planet now than any other time in history. In fact, according to the US Census Bureau, it is estimated that when Jesus was born, there were only about 200 million people on the planet. From the time of Christ to just two hundred years ago in 1804, the population grew to 1 billion people. Just think about that. It took well over two thousand years for the world population to reach 1 billion.[1]

Then population growth began to accelerate. What took more than 2,000 years to accomplish took only 123 years to duplicate. By 1927 the world's population was at 2 billion. Due to advances in medicine, technology, and agriculture, mortality rates dropped, and the biggest population increase in human history was taking shape. In 33 short years (by 1960), we racked in another billion people. And since then we have rapidly made our way to 7 billion people at the time of this writing. We have more than doubled the global population since just 1960.[2]

If you were born in the sixties, there are twice as many people on the planet today as there were when you were born. Throughout human history global population growth stayed minimal and steady. Then all of a sudden, in a very short amount of time, the number of people on the earth exploded!

That is incredible! No generation that has ever lived before you had the potential to reach as many people as you do right now at this moment in your life. God destined for there to be mass numbers of people alive on the planet in your lifetime! The greatest potential for revival exists in your generation. The greatest harvest known to mankind exists now.

I wake up every day amazed by that possibility. Not only are we being set up for the greatest revival the world has ever seen, but also we wake up every day with the biggest, fattest spiritual bank account of anyone who has ever lived before us. It's as if we're the recipients of an incredible spiritual trust fund. We have inherited generation after generation of promise, prayer, and breakthrough.

Just think about the fact that two thousand years ago Jesus taught mankind to pray, "Our Father in heaven, hallowed be Your Name. Your kingdom come. Your will be done on earth as it is in heaven" (Matt. 6:9–10, NKJV). What a powerful prayer. It is the heart and passion of God to release His kingdom on the earth, and He wanted us to partner in prayer with Him to see it happen. Now, just imagine how many times that prayer has been prayed. All over the world, in every language, by multitudes of people, martyrs, children, kings, missionaries, priests, men, women, slaves, leaders—the collective voice of the lovers and followers of Christ together throughout history have joined their prayer with the prayer of Jesus.

For centuries that powerful prayer has been prayed over and over again. The bowls of intercession in heaven are full to overflowing, and heaven is longing, looking for those on whom they can be poured out. At this very moment, as you're reading this, all of heaven is postured to pour out the answer to that prayer in and through your life. "Your kingdom come. Your will be done on earth as it is in heaven!"

God wants to release His kingdom (His life, love, healing, peace, joy, resolution, freedom, provision, and so on) in your life and through your life to the whole world! At this very moment—not because of anything spectacular you've done but simply if you've said yes to God's free gift of salvation—you have been born into the family of God and become the recipient of every good thing in the kingdom, including the legacy of thousands of years of prayer, obedience, sacrifice, worship, and promise left by those who have gone before you. It is now yours to walk in today.

So not only are we being set up for the greatest revival the earth has ever seen, but we also have everything we need to see it happen! We lack nothing. We are sons and daughters of the King and possess full access to everything we need to bring God's kingdom to earth. As we walk in union with God, He fills us with Himself. And as we choose to love those around us, everything He has put in us will spill out and transform those we touch.

FROM SLAVE TO ROYALTY

S EVERAL YEARS AGO I had a vision during a time of prayer that deeply impacted my life. In the vision I saw myself as a young child. The first scene was very dark, very sad. I was an orphan and a slave. I was chained together with millions of other people—too numerous to count—and we were all so full of pain and sadness. We were walking somberly on our way to our death. It was a horrible scene.

Then, suddenly, we passed in front of a gorgeous castle. The castle was enormous, glorious, and full of vibrant colors. It was unlike anything I had ever seen before. As we neared the castle, the large doors opened, and out walked the most regal and beautiful king I had ever seen. He looked so strong yet so kind and inviting. I desperately wanted to be near him, but I knew it was impossible.

I couldn't take my eyes off him; his beauty mesmerized me. Everything in me wanted to run to this person I didn't even know. I was only a child, but he just seemed so safe, so perfect. I wished desperately to be near him. But that seemed impossible. I was just one small person in a sea of people.

The king began to walk through the multitudes of people, and he seemed to be moving in my direction. My heart started pounding, but I knew he would never see me—I was just an orphan, a slave, and a little girl at that. He continued to press through the crowd, and I couldn't help but hope desperately that just maybe he would see me. Then it happened. His big warm eyes met mine, and he walked right up to me. He got down on his knees to be eye level with me; then he looked deep into my eyes and said, "You! I choose you! I want to be your daddy. Would you like to be my little girl?"

I couldn't believe what I was hearing! I squealed a hearty, "Yes!", and jumped into his arms. I couldn't believe this was happening to me. It was like a dream come true. I was going to have a father. I wasn't going to be a slave. I didn't have to die! So many things were rushing through my head as he broke the chains off my feet and carried me into the castle. As we entered the castle, my senses were overwhelmed. There were objects, colors, smells, and sounds that were so glorious yet foreign to me. I had never seen anything like this. It hardly even seemed real.

There were endless hallways inside, and each hallway had endless doors. Without being told, I just knew that behind each door was something like a world of its own. I knew that behind one door was enough food to feed the whole world. Behind another door there was creativity for every song, dance, business, project, and so forth in the whole world. Behind one door was all the money you could ever need. Behind another was all the medicine and healing you could ever need. It just went on and on. This place was endless; it lacked nothing. I could spend my whole life opening new doors and never even see half of it. I was shocked by what I was seeing.

As we entered the castle, the king ordered some maids to get me cleaned up. The maids were so kind and attentive. I felt so loved. They prepared a bubble bath for me, and as they bathed me, they told me all about how life as a slave gets you dirty, but in this new place all that dirt gets washed away and you are cleansed. Then they dried me up and examined some wounds I had on my body. They talked about how life as an orphan oftentimes leaves people with wounds, but that I shouldn't worry because in this place they had ointments to heal me, and I wouldn't have any of those pains anymore. After they put healing ointments on my wounds, the maids dressed me in the most breathtaking gown I had ever seen. I looked in the mirror and hardly recognized myself. I couldn't believe this was really happening to me.

Once I was dressed, the maids walked me back out to the king. He lovingly looked at me, visibly happy about my new appearance, and he came over and got down on his knees in front of me once again and began to speak to me lovingly. He said, "Today I am truly adopting you as my daughter. You are now royalty. We must get one thing straight. You are no longer allowed to talk like a slave, think like a slave, or act like a slave. That is not who you are. You are the daughter of the High King, and you must learn how to live as royalty. Look around you! All of this, everything you see, is now your home. You have freedom to go anywhere and to use everything here."

I was speechless. He then smiled and said, "I have a gift for you! Open up your hand." I opened my hand, and in the palm of my hand he placed a key. It looked like an ancient key. It looked well used but beautiful. He told me, "With this key you can go anywhere in this house. Welcome home!" The joy on his face was so life-giving. Instantly I somehow knew inside of me that the key was faith. Faith was the key that allowed me to open up every single door in the kingdom. Faith would unlock everything in this place, and I had the key in my hand.

When the vision ended, I sat speechless for quite a long time. It all suddenly made sense. In fact, before I had the vision, I was actually complaining to God, telling Him that I wished I had a "cool testimony." You know, something dramatic and powerful to share with people. I have loved Jesus as long as I can remember, and although the path had some bumps along the way, I've walked with Him my whole life. It was after my complaining to God about my testimony that I heard Him say, "I'll show you the power of your testimony," and then I was taken into this vision.

This is the power of our testimony! We were slaves, we were orphans, we were sentenced to death, and we were brought into the kingdom of light and cleansed and healed and turned into royalty! There is nothing more powerful than that! Ever since that encounter more than ten years ago, I still hear the Lord whisper into my heart, "Don't think like a slave. Don't talk like a slave. Don't act like a slave. That is not who you are. You are royalty." For most of us, this is quite a process—a process of transformation that doesn't always happen overnight. It takes years of retraining to not respond to situations like a slave or an orphan.

For many, this will be the biggest challenge in their life. I think that is why we are told that all of creation is groaning in intercession for us, for the sons of God to come forth. It's not always an easy transition to live like a son or daughter of God. But the amazing thing is that when we truly take

Him at His word and realize that we are wholeheartedly adopted and loved, and that we have access to everything in the kingdom, everything changes in that moment.

We have been given the key that unlocks everything in the kingdom. That key is faith. Faith is the giant magnet that pulls down all the blessings from heaven to the earth. By faith we access everything in the kingdom of God. I'm sure you've noticed by now that seeing promises in the Bible doesn't automatically mean those things suddenly appear in your life. Those blessings are activated through faith. Faith is the key.

God is bringing His children into the understanding that we're truly adopted and that it's time for us to stop living in spiritual poverty. It's time for the sons and daughters of God to come forth and to shine!

> In love he predestined us to be adopted as his sons through Jesus Christ, in accordance with his pleasure and will.
>
> —EPHESIANS 1:4–5

WHO ARE THE MASSES?

W E KNOW GOD has allowed the largest harvest field to emerge in our generation (a whopping 7 billion people). I fully believe He has saved it for this time because we are equipped with what we need to reach this harvest (resources, technology, years of intercession, and so on). But *who* are the 7 billion people out there whom God has divinely set up for the world's greatest revival? Who are the 7 billion people whom God has positioned to come into the knowledge of who He is? Who are the masses we pray for when we intercede for revival? Who are the souls all of heaven is interceding for and passionately pursuing? As royalty and ambassadors of that heavenly kingdom, it's important that we understand *who* we're talking about if we're going to be effective in our evangelism, discipleship, and church planting.

According to 2011 United Nations statistics, of the 7 billion people alive today, roughly 1.85 billion (somewhere near 27 percent) are children under the age of fifteen. In addition, there are another 1.2 billion youth between the ages of fifteen and twenty-four. That means approximately 3 billion people on the planet are children and youth! That's nearly half (roughly 43 percent) of the global population![1]

A huge percentage of the people on the planet are children and youth! Some may find that statistic rather shocking, especially when oftentimes in the church most of our evangelism, discipleship, ministry, church planting, sermons, programs, and leadership training target adults. So much of what we do and talk about in the church is adult-focused. Many of us may not readily admit that since we make sure our churches have Sunday school programs and that we send our youth off to youth camp. But in many circles the value and depth of what we are sowing into our children and youth is not equivalent to what we sow into the adults.

Here is one simple example of this: the majority of Sunday school programs use a basic, generic curriculum for their children's programs. I don't have a problem with curriculum. I believe it can be very helpful. But what if the senior pastor of the church decided that for the next five years he wasn't going to spend the time during the week to seek God for a timely word for the body but would instead just pull his sermons from the Internet each week. Many church members would likely feel offended, devalued, and unimpressed.

We expect our spiritual leaders to put forth effort and prayer to share with us what they sense is on God's heart for our congregation. We expect them to teach from a place of passion and experience. For whatever reason this value doesn't always translate to the church's care for our younger brothers and sisters in the Lord. We may not provide our children's leaders with the resources or expect them to provide the same level of spiritual leadership adults may anticipate.

What if instead we cultivated a culture where ministry to children was seen as vital, powerful, and worthy of much time and attention? What if from a young age children were being trained in the deep things of the Lord and being raised up to truly know Christ and to live wholeheartedly in the kingdom?

What if ministering to children was seen as a high calling, worthy of great value and honor? What if churches demonstrated their commitment to children by giving finances, time, and space to this area of ministry? And what if those who shepherded our children led them with deep commitment and passion? Who would these children be twenty years from now if from a young age they had been exposed to and led into a deep, passionate relationship with Christ? If from a young age they knew their Father's voice and walked close to His heart? What if the supernatural was just "natural" for them? How much pain would they be spared on their journey? What kinds of lives would they be living in their twenties, thirties, forties, fifties? What kinds of lives would they be living right now?

There is no differentiation in the Spirit. Just like adults, children do not have to "earn" their spiritual authority. If we live in a church culture where one must "earn" his or her spiritual authority, we will spend our whole lives striving, performing, jumping through religious political hoops, and emptying the cross of the power it delivers.

It doesn't matter if you are five years old or fifty—if you are born again, you are brought into the fullness of Christ and His kingdom. We are filled with the same Holy Spirit. Children do not get a junior Holy Spirit. Yes, children may not have the emotional maturity that someone older may possess, but when you look at Scripture, that fact never seemed to bother Jesus. He chose the uneducated, outcasts, emotionally driven, and seemingly disqualified to be the closest to Him. In fact, He even said:

> I tell you the truth, unless you change and become like little children, you will never enter the kingdom of heaven. Therefore, whoever humbles himself like this child is the greatest in the kingdom of heaven.
>
> —MATTHEW 18:3–4

Sometimes some of the biggest spirits reside in some of the smallest bodies. We know that a large percentage of the global population is young—very young, in fact—but what else do we need to know about these masses of people alive in our generation? According to the US Census Bureau, 60 percent of the world's population lives in Asia, 15 percent lives in Africa, 11 percent lives in Europe, 9 percent in Latin America and the Caribbean, and only 5 percent in North America.[2]

It's important to understand that the masses of people God wants to encounter in our day are "out there." There is a harvest field in every nation, but if God has great love and an incredible plan for every person in the world—just imagine how much He wants to do right now in Asia (considering 60 percent of the world lives there). God sees the big picture—and so should we. We in North America make up a very small percentage of the world.

If we are to be effective in releasing God's kingdom on the earth, we must understand that the masses of people alive today are "out there," young, and one more thing—poor.

According to the World Bank, in 2001 some 2.7 billion people lived on less than two dollars a day.[3] That means one out of three people in the world is suffering extreme poverty.

(Just imagine if every third person you knew was suffering like this.) And of the 2.4 billion children out there right now who are age nineteen and younger, half of them are living in poverty.[4] Half of the world's children are just trying to survive every day. Just think for a moment of all the painful things that come along with extreme poverty—no access to clean water, sickness, hunger, pain, no education, homelessness, and death. Half of our children have to deal with these things every single day.

I am so confident that God is not intimidated by these statistics but instead has a beautiful plan of redemption, and all of heaven is working to release that plan on the earth! I believe regardless of what each of us feels called to in our lives, we must take into consideration the Great Commission and the harvest God is putting before us. We must examine that harvest field and intelligently and prayerfully seek God for strategies.

MAKING SPACE FOR CHILDREN

My question then is, if we do not have a paradigm shift in our churches, how relevant and effective will we be in our generation? Also, who is better suited to reach the masses of children alive today than the very children and youth who fill our churches? *Children are not the church of tomorrow; they are the church of today*—and we must start empowering and releasing them as such. We can no longer send the kids off to play in their classrooms, do a little craft, and have a snack while the adults have "real church." That kind of thinking is dangerous. Not only will it weaken the powerful children God has sent us, but it will also cripple our whole body.

About ten years ago I had a vision that was both disturbing and enlightening. As I was praying, I began to see a picture of a bride who was standing some distance from me. The bride was too far away for me to see the details of her body and face. In the vision I started moving closer toward her and was taken aback by what I saw. She was deformed.

It was bizarre because nothing seemed to actually be wrong with her, but nearly half of her body was atrophied and crippled simply from not being used. All of the muscles and flesh on half of her body were sagging and shriveled up. I gasped, thinking how unlovely she looked. She could barely move. She needed a lot of help to do basic things. I felt so sad for her, because her mobility was so very limited.

The vision ended there, and I sat for a long time contemplating and praying about what I had seen. I knew God was trying to show me something, but I just didn't understand. Then He spoke in that still, small voice that can sometimes be piercingly loud and said, "When children and youth aren't empowered to function within the body and aren't being used and valued, My bride is left looking like this." I hardly knew how to respond. It's true that no one can know exactly how many children are in the body of Christ. But judging from human population statistics alone, it's safe to say that nearly half of the body of Christ may be made up of children and youth. (In fact, most of us would agree that we know more children who genuinely have faith in God than adults!)

That is an incredible thought: potentially half of the body of Christ is children and youth! Just let that sink in a little bit. There are so many scriptures that talk about the body working together and there being unity among believers.

But so many adult believers fail to see that the members of the body of Christ include children and youth! If the bride is going to be beautiful and powerful and effective, we must teach the adult arm to work together with the child arm, and the adult eye to see together with the child's eye. We must learn to utilize all of our muscles and value each member for what he or she brings to the table.

In our culture it's common to believe that we adults have something to teach the children and that we should instruct them so one day they can contribute to the kingdom. But we are missing a huge piece of the puzzle with that kind of thinking. Yes, it is absolutely true that we need to teach and train children. But children already bring something to the table. They are already carrying God's DNA, and we need them—not just later, but now!

We need them, and they need us. We are a body, and we can be the best version of ourselves only when we make space and have value for one another. The bride needs to be unified and healed so she no longer has to be limited and weak.

27
GENERATIONAL UNITY—THE KEY TO GLOBAL REVIVAL

J
OHN 17 CAPTURES such a precious piece of Jesus's heart for us. In His last prayer before going to the cross, Jesus prays for you and me.

> My prayer is not for them alone. I pray also for those who will believe in me through their message, that all of them may be one, Father, just as you are in me and I am in you. May they also be in us so that the world may believe that you have sent me. I have given them the glory that you gave me, that they may be one as we are one: I in them and you in me. May they be brought to complete unity to let the world know that you sent me and have loved them even as you have loved me.
>
> —JOHN 17:20–23

Jesus prayed for unity. Union. Togetherness. What amazes me about this prayer is the promise hidden in the midst of it: "Father, just as you are in me and I am in you. May they also be in us *so that the world may believe* you have sent me." Then again in verse 23, "*to let the world know...*" When we figure out how to walk in union with God and with one another, something happens. The world is provoked to belief.

I'm not sure if you're hearing what I'm hearing! If we can

come into alignment with this type of unity Jesus is praying about, it will unlock belief in 7 billion people. That is called global revival! That is called the greatest harvest the world has ever seen! This type of union Jesus is praying about is not a major key—it is the key to starting a global revival, union with God and union with one another. Without going into a major teaching on unity, I think we can look at some of the primary themes in Jesus's prayer. I see three obvious levels of unity Jesus is praying for us to enter into.

Unity with God. Jesus prayed, "May they also be in us" (v. 21), then He said in verse 23, "I in them and you in me." God wants to fill us with Himself, and He wants us to remain in Him. Mankind was created for this type of union with God. God wants to be in us, and He wants us to be in Him. When we walk in true union with God, we become co-creators. We start to look like Jesus, and the world takes notice.

Unity among all believers everywhere. In verses 20–21 Jesus said, "My prayer is not for them alone. I pray also for those who will believe in me through their message, that all of them may be one." And in verse 22 Jesus says, "That they may be one as we are one." Jesus understood the power of unity among believers and knew it was a key to unlock belief in the world. Jesus prayed that all who believe in Him would be united, that we would be "one."

Sadly, Christians have found this to be one of our greatest challenges. For some odd reason we've bought the lie that we can be united only with those who interpret Scripture the same way we do. Hence, there are literally thousands of different Christian denominations. The true spirit of unity doesn't exist simply because everyone thinks the same or agrees. True unity recognizes and embraces our differences but chooses to honor and love above all else. The unity Jesus is talking about is far more concerned with loving one another and working together than simply agreeing on something.

Unity among generations. In verse 21 Jesus prayed, "That all of them may be one, Father, just as you are in me and I am in you. May they also be in us so that the world may believe." This is the prayer of a Son speaking to His Father, a Son who has walked in perfect unity with His Father, a Son who in John 17:10 says to His Father, "All I have is yours, and all you have is mine." Jesus wants to see you and me walk in the same generational unity He and His Father walk in— the sons and the fathers united together so the world may believe.

Jesus prayed, "Father, just as you are in me and I am in you" (v. 21). That is a crazy prayer! Jesus used the words "just as," not "kind of like" or "similar to." The Son asked the Father that we would be one just as He and the Father are one. To really understand the magnitude of what Jesus is asking for we have to examine what His relationship with the Father looked like while He was on the earth.

First of all, before Jesus even started His ministry, the Father extravagantly and generously demonstrated His commitment and pleasure over His Son, as we see at Jesus's baptism.

> Then Jesus came from Galilee to the Jordan to be baptized by John. But John tried to deter him, saying, "I need to be baptized by you, and do you come to me?" Jesus replied, "Let it be so now; it is proper for us to do this to fulfill all righteousness." Then John consented. As soon as Jesus was baptized, he went up out of the

> water. At that moment heaven was opened, and he saw the Spirit of God descending like a dove and lighting on him. And a voice from heaven said, "This is my Son, whom I love; with him I am well pleased."
>
> —MATTHEW 3:13–17

This is a pretty bold and passionate move by the Father. The Father was intent on letting everyone know that He loved His Son and that His Son had His approval. From that point on the Father continually backed up and exalted His Son. The Father demonstrated His approval of Jesus performing miracles and signs and wonders through Him. Again, in Matthew 17, God roars His resounding support of His Son from heaven.

> While he was still speaking, a bright cloud enveloped them, and a voice from the cloud said, "This is my Son, whom I love; with him I am well pleased. Listen to him!" When the disciples heard this, they fell facedown to the ground, terrified.
>
> —MATTHEW 17:5–6

In case anybody missed it the first time, the Father bellows from heaven audibly through a cloud and says, "This is my Son....Listen to him!" The intensity of the experience leaves the disciples facedown and terrified. Long before Jesus physically took form on the earth, the Father had been talking about His Son, making a way for Him and preparing people for His coming. Then the Father allowed the Son to fully represent Him on the earth. He gave Him supreme authority, saying every knee would bow to Him and every tongue would confess that He was Lord.

Your attitude should be the same as that of Christ Jesus: *Who, being in very nature God*, did not consider equality with God something to be grasped, but made himself nothing, taking the very nature of a servant, being made in human likeness. And being found in appearance as a man, he humbled himself and became obedient to death—even death on a cross! Therefore God exalted him to the highest place and gave him the name that is above every name, that at the name of Jesus every knee should bow, in heaven and on earth and under the earth, and every tongue confess that Jesus Christ is Lord, to the glory of God the Father.

—PHILIPPIANS 2:5–11, EMPHASIS ADDED

The Father fully made a way for His Son. He backed Him up in power. He refused to do anything without Him—and instead made Him the center and the path to Himself. Then He exalted Him to the highest place and gave Him the name that is above every name! *Wow!* That is a radical demonstration of a loving and generous Father.

WALKING HAND IN HAND

Let's look at how Jesus interacted with the Father. In the Philippian passage we see that Jesus, although He had every right to access the benefits of being God, walked in absolute servanthood and humility. He always directed people to the Father; He lived and breathed to point people to the Father. He refused to do things alone but walked closely connected to the Father. Jesus didn't live for His own will. He lived for His Father's will. He taught us to pray, "Your kingdom come, your will be done on earth as it is in heaven" (Matt. 6:10).

Then again in Luke 22:42 He prays to the Father saying, "Yet not my will, but yours be done."

Jesus lived to honor and exalt the Father in everything He did! He wasn't trying to build a name for Himself. He gave every ounce of Himself to demonstrate to people how good and beautiful His Father is. Jesus lived so connected to His Father, He would steal away from the masses to press into His Daddy's heart and draw His strength from that place. He lived to please and honor His Father.

Both the Father and Son were passionate about each other—seeing, loving, serving the other above Himself. They refused to do anything without the other, but hand in hand they walked. Their relationship is our model of what true generational unity should look like. And this beautiful, mutually honoring relationship is what Jesus prayed you and I would have as well. Jesus prayed that as fathers and sons, mothers and daughters we would walk in this same manner—refusing to do things alone, always making a way for the other, serving, backing up, putting our approval and affection on display, and seeking the will of the other. In fact, He went as far as to say "just as"—"that all of them may be one, Father, *just as* you are in me and I am in you" (John 17:21, emphasis added).

The Father and the Son needed to walk in complete unity so that the world could come into belief. I believe the same holds true for us. God is awakening us to the vital need for fathers and sons, mothers and daughters to learn to walk in such generational unity that the world is provoked to belief. Jesus was able to confidently make the statement in John 10:30, "I and the Father are one." I pray that we too will be able to boldly make that statement and that we would walk as one across generational lines.

> See, I will send you the prophet Elijah before that great and dreadful day of the LORD comes. He will turn the hearts of the fathers to their children, and the hearts of the children to their fathers; or else I will come and strike the land with a curse.
>
> —MALACHI 4:5–6

A TREE AND A CHAINSAW

28

ONG BEFORE I began working with children, I had a vision that really impacted me. In the vision I saw a large, beautiful tree, and around the tree was a group of spiritual leaders (pastors, ministers, elders, and so on). In the vision I could see that these leaders were trying to figure out how to cut down the tree. After some consideration they pulled out some small plastic knives used for eating and began using them to cut through the tree.

As an observer of this I could see how ridiculous the notion was. There was no way they were ever going to get the tree down with those flimsy plastic knives. Suddenly I realized that at the base of the tree—right near their feet—was a chainsaw. Totally confused as to why they wouldn't use the chainsaw instead, I spoke up and said, "Why don't you just use the chainsaw?"

Some rolled their eyes at my suggestion, and some continued to work as if they didn't even hear me. Then I was flooded with comments such as: "We're perfectly fine without that!" "Chainsaws are too noisy—they give me a headache!" "Chainsaws are heavy and make you dirty!" "Chainsaws are just annoying and too much work!" They soldiered on, looking very dignified as they continued their pathetic attempt to chop down a tree with plastic knives. I was at a total loss. I could not for the life of me understand their logic. Then the vision ended.

I spent quite a lot of time seeking God about the meaning of the vision. I knew God was speaking something to me, and I didn't want to miss it. Finally the Lord gave me the interpretation. He explained that the tree represented the kingdom of God. Everyone was working to bring the kingdom to earth. The tree falling represented promises fulfilled and kingdom activity being released in the natural—the tree falling was a great thing and something that God desired to happen. Yet the leaders in my vision were comfortable and had a particular view of how they wanted to do things. They continued to use the same (and only) method they knew to use, even though it was unsuccessful.

I was eager to know what the chainsaw represented since it was integral to the vision. The Lord showed me that the chainsaw represented children and youth—they are the "power tool." I sat in silence trying to soak that in and understand what exactly that meant. I began to realize that a chainsaw, although an extremely effective and powerful tool, cannot do anything by itself. The chainsaw is only able to do its job when it is safely held in the hands of an experienced adult. In fact, a chainsaw can be very dangerous if not used correctly, but nothing works better to chop down a tree.

It all made sense. Children and youth truly are power tools in the kingdom of God. God has given them a faith that is unmatched and a purity and simplicity that attracts heaven. I wholeheartedly believe that when children are given freedom to be all God has created them to be, and are safely led and held in the hands of wise fathers and mothers, that tree will fall—but only because we are all walking together. Generational unity is the key. One thing I found interesting was the response of the leaders in my vision. Obviously these leaders do not reflect all the ministers in the body of Christ, but I think God was allowing me to see a mind-set present in some leaders that is preventing God from moving.

I've heard so many people tell me, "I'm just not called to children! That is just not my thing!" Or, "No, thank you! Working with kids is too much work!" Or, "They're crazy! I get a headache!" Yes, not everyone is passionate about working with children and has the patience needed to teach them, and that's OK. But not working with kids isn't an option, unless you're willing to be ineffective and divisive in the body of Christ. Children are our partners in our service to the Lord. Children are powerful tools and are very effective at releasing the kingdom when walking arm in arm with trusted adults.

We must make sure we never allow ourselves to subtly buy the lie that adults are the real stakeholders in the church and that children are just "playing church" or "in training." Together we are the church. Together God has given each one of us a vital role to play in releasing God's kingdom on earth. When we learn to walk in unity, that tree will quickly fall!

29

A RECURRING DREAM

FROM THE AGE of fifteen until I was about twenty-one, I had a recurring dream. I had never in my life had a recurring dream before that time and haven't had one since. But for seven years I kept having the same dream over and over again. It haunted me. I wanted desperately to know what it meant or what God wanted me to do with it. The dream was simple and went like this.

It's late at night, and I'm sitting in the backseat of some type of car or taxi, riding through the city streets heading somewhere. Gazing out the window, I suddenly notice a small body lying in the gutter. I scream to the driver to stop the car. My heart is pounding. When he stops, I jump out of the car and run to the body. It's a little baby lying helplessly in the gutter, abandoned and malnourished. I'm very aware in the dream that time is of the essence and that if something isn't done immediately, this baby will starve to death within moments. I panic. I look around, but it's late at night and the area is deserted. There is nowhere to take the baby and nothing to do to give her nourishment. I know there are only seconds left. In absolute desperation I draw the baby to my breast and pray for God to supernaturally flow through me. Supernaturally milk starts to flow, and I'm able to nurse the baby. The baby is rescued and survives. The dream ends.

Over and over again for seven years I had the same dream, same baby, same ending. Now as a mother of three, the idea of nursing a baby doesn't seem bizarre. But at age fifteen it was weird. For years I really wrestled with the meaning of this dream. I knew it had meaning for me personally but also for the body of Christ at large. One day at age twenty-one I felt the Lord speak to me about the meaning of the dream. He said there was a generation on the brink of starvation. A generation that was a gift and a promise had been "abandoned" and "neglected" in a sense, and they desperately needed to be nourished. God was looking for people who in the midst of their busy lives—en route to wherever they were headed—would notice, would see this starving generation, and would be willing to stop, even if it was in the middle of the night and they were tired.

I felt like God was releasing a promise in the dream for those who are willing to stop. Even if you feel you have absolutely nothing to give and you've never done anything like that before, if you will draw these little ones close to you, God will supernaturally flow through you to nourish a generation back to life in a way you never imagined was possible. After I received the revelation of that dream, I never had the dream again.

I can testify that through the years I have seen God fulfill the promise He laid out in the dream. I have seen so many different people around the world who felt inadequate or totally out of their element when they accepted the challenge to minister to children. As they embraced a hungry generation, God supernaturally began to use them to feed these precious little ones. God is simply looking for someone who will take the time to stop and see and care. He does the rest, and it's beautiful.

THE 4/14 WINDOW—THE GOLDEN
AGE OF OPPORTUNITY

Y OU'VE LIKELY HEARD of the 10/40 Window. It's a term
that was coined by missionary strategist Luis Bush in
1990 referring to the regions of the eastern hemisphere
10 degrees and 40 degrees north of the equator, stretching from
North Africa across China. The 10/40 Window contains the
largest population of non-Christians and has the least access to
the gospel coupled with great socioeconomic challenges. Bush's
campaign to mobilize people to pray for this region truly was
a catalytic effort to get the global church to embrace the Great
Commission and streamline evangelistic efforts. The concept
revolutionized the missions movement.

In recent years Bush has come on the scene again and
urged missions movements around the world to embrace a
new missional focus: the 4/14 Window. The 10/40 Window
referenced a geographic frame; the 4/14 Window describes
a demographic frame—a life season comprising the years
between ages four and fourteen. In recent years this period
of time in the lifespan of a child has quickly become known
as the golden age of opportunity.

Several statistics have emerged through the years that
have radically shifted evangelism efforts. Missiologist Bryant

Myers, former director of World Vision's MARC Ministries, reported in the early 1990s that nearly 85 percent of people became Christians between the ages of four and fourteen.[1] More recent research points to a similar trend. In 2004 the Barna Research Group conducted a national survey in the United States and found that American children between the ages of five and thirteen have a 32 percent probability of accepting Christ, while teenagers between the ages of fourteen and eighteen have only a 4 percent probability, and adults age nineteen and older have a 6 percent probability. The extensive Barna research also indicates that the age at which a person accepts Christ as his Savior is related to various attributes of his spiritual life. For example, people who become Christians before their teen years are more likely to remain "absolutely committed" to Christianity than those converted when they are older.[2]

"What you believe at age 13 is pretty much what you're going to die believing," said Barna, author of *Transforming Children Into Spiritual Champions*. His research also shows that children's ministry is an ideal time to shape the church's next generation of leaders. In a 2003 Barna Group nationwide survey of pastors, church staff, and lay leaders, four of five leaders said they participated in church children's programs for a number of years before they turned thirteen.[3]

The research unanimously points to one thing: children between the ages of four and fourteen are the ripest, most fruitful harvest field on the planet. It is estimated that there are somewhere around 1.2 billion children currently in the 4/14 Window. This truly is a golden age of opportunity. This knowledge about the 4/14 Window is shifting missions movements around the world. In discussing his recently written booklet about the 4/14 Window, Bush stated:

> This booklet is an urgent appeal to consider the strategic importance and potential of the 1.2 billion children and youth in the 4/14 Window. It is a plea to open your heart and mind to the idea of reaching and raising up a new generation from within that vast group—a generation that can experience personal transformation and can be mobilized as agents for transformation throughout the world. Our vision and hope is to maximize their transformational impact while they are young, and to mobilize them for continuing impact for the rest of their lives. I invite you to join with many others who are making a commitment to fulfill this vision and realize this hope.
>
> To maximize the transformational impact of children and youth in the 4/14 Window we must address the spiritual, mental, physical, relational, economic, and social issues they face. We must also confront their "ministerial poverty"—the scarcity of opportunities for them to exercise their gifts and achieve their potential in ways that honor God and advance His Kingdom.
>
> It is crucial that mission efforts be re-prioritized and re-directed toward the 4–14 age group worldwide. This requires that we become acutely aware of what is taking place in their lives. We must also endeavor to understand their nature and the essential means to nurture them. Only with this kind of informed awareness will we be able to reach them, shape them, and raise them up to transform the world.[4]

I couldn't agree with Luis more. I believe those in the 4/14 Window are not only extremely ripe for salvation, but they also are the ones we should be training up and releasing to reach their peers and friends. The Barna Group has also done extensive studies on which types of evangelism efforts receive the greatest response. Children in the 4/14 Window don't typically respond to crusades, television evangelism, or church altar calls. The highest response comes when a friend or family member shares Christ with them. We have to pay attention and focus our efforts appropriately. The harvest is plentiful and the workers are few, but it doesn't have to be that way!

> Then he said to his disciples, "The harvest is plentiful but the workers are few. Ask the Lord of the harvest, therefore, to send out workers into his harvest field."
> —MATTHEW 9:37–38

The harvest is so plentiful! We must ask ourselves, why are the workers few? Is it because we don't have enough missionaries and evangelists in the world? Christianity is the largest religion in the world. It's estimated that about one-third of people worldwide profess to be Christians.[5] If every Christian in the world led two people to the Lord, the whole world would be saved. So it's not that there's a shortage of Christians to do the work. We must ask ourselves, then, why the workers are so few.

I'm sure there are a variety of factors that contribute to the situation, but I believe one of the important ones is that few people are really targeting the primary harvest field: children. Having worked with hundreds of churches and children's pastors, I have learned very quickly that it's almost like pulling teeth to get anybody to work with the kids. Children's pastors are overworked and desperate for help, trying to rely on inconsistent volunteers and often left feeling alone and unsupported. Many times working with children is seen as a starting point from which one hopes to quickly graduate, first by moving on to work with youth then the "real church," the adults.

Another factor to consider is that I believe our most effective workers (our power tools) aren't being raised up and released into the harvest field. Children between the ages of four and fourteen are our most powerful untapped resource in the body of Christ. What would happen if all over the world we equipped and mobilized our children to bring life and love to their peers? Yes, the harvest is very plentiful—especially in our generation. In fact, it has never before been as plentiful as it is now. And, yes, to date the workers have been few. But that is shifting.

God is raising up passionate children just like the ones you've read about in this book—children who love Him wholeheartedly and long to share His love with those they meet. God is raising up an army of harvesters unlike anything we've seen before. For years people have been praying to the Lord of the harvest, asking Him to send out workers into the field, and He has heard their cry and is doing it.

Children are not only the church of today, but they also are the missionaries of today and the evangelists of today. I pray that each one of us will have eyes to see what God is doing and the willingness to get behind it. God is setting the world up for revival in our generation. And at the same time,

He has filled the earth with young souls who know Him and love Him passionately. The Lord of the harvest has heard the prayers of the saints, and He has responded. He has sent a child to lead them.

NOTES

Chapter 4
A Butterfly, a Breakthrough, and Angels

1. Jumo's name has been changed to protect his identity.
2. Mary's name has been changed to protect her identity.

Chapter 5
A Date With Jesus

1. Megan Scotney in discussion with the author, August 2011. Used with her parents' permission.
2. Ibid.

Chapter 7
Conner's Encounter

1. Ben Armstrong, in discussion with the author, June 2011.

Chapter 10
When Prayers Shake Darkness

1. Pastor Patrick Siabuta, in discussion with the author, July 2011.

Chapter 24
The Divine Setup

1. US Census Bureau, "Historical Estimates of World Population," http://www.census.gov/population/international/data/idb/worldhis.php (accessed January 19, 2012); United Nations, "The World at Six Billion," Table 1: "World Population From Year 0 to Stabilization," 1999, http://www.un.org/esa/population/publications/sixbillion/sixbilpart1.pdf (accessed January 19, 2012).
2. United Nations, "The World at Six Billion," Table 1: "World Population From Year 0 to Stabilization."

Chapter 26
Who Are the Masses?

1. Population Division, Population Estimates and Projections Section, "World Population Prospects, the 2010 Revision," United Nations, Department of Economic and Social Affairs, June 28, 2011,

http://esa.un.org/wpp/Excel-Data/population.htm (accessed January 20, 2012).

2. Population Division, Department of Economic and Social Affairs, *World Population Prospects: The 2010 Revision* (New York: United Nations, 2011), "Table I.2," http://esa.un.org/unpd/wpp/ Documentation/pdf/WPP2010_Highlights.pdf (accessed January 20, 2012).

3. As reported by the United Nations in "The International Day for the Eradication of Poverty: 17 October," http://www.un.org/esa/ socdev/poverty/images/IDEP_flyer.pdf (accessed January 23, 2012).

4. Population Division, Department of Economic and Social Affairs, *World Population Prospects: The 2010 Revision*; United Nations Children's Fund, State of the World's Children 2005 (New York: UNICF, 2004), http://www.unicef.org/sowc05/english/sowc05 .pdf (accessed February 17, 2012).

Chapter 30
The 4/14 Window—the Golden Age of Opportunity

1. Dan Brewster, "The '4/14 Window': Child Ministries and Mission Strategies," Compassion International, updated August 2005, http://www.compassion.com/multimedia/The%204_14%20Window .pdf (accessed March 5, 2012).

2. George Barna, *Transforming Children Into Spiritual Champions* (Ventura, CA: Regal, 2003), 33–34.

3. John W. Kennedy, "The 4-14 Window," *Christianity Today*, July 1, 2004, http://www.christianitytoday.com/ct/2004/july/37.53.html (accessed April 25, 2012).

4. Luis Bush, *Raising Up a New Generation From the 4/14 Window to Transform the World* (Flushing, NY: 4/14 Window Global Initiative, 2011), 3, http://4to14window.com/4-14-window -booklet (accessed January 23, 2012).

5. AFP, "US Study Says Christians One Third of World Population," December 19, 2011, http://ph.news.yahoo.com/one-third -world-embrace-christianity-us-study-184225932.html (accessed February 17, 2012).

ABOUT THE AUTHOR

Jennifer and her husband Jonatan live in Los Angeles, CA with their three children Malaika, Josiah, and Ruah. Both Jonatan and Jennifer serve as Senior Associate Pastors at Expression 58 Ministries, a church and regional ministry they helped to plant which champions love, creativity, and justice in the heart of the culture capital. In addition, Jennifer is the Founder and President of Global Children's Movement, an international not-for-profit organization that is committed to mercy and justice on behalf of children around the world. With passion to bring both natural and spiritual resolution to global issues, their projects include: holistic schools in war zones, homes for children rescued out of the sex trade, home for orphaned and abandoned children, ministry to incarcerated youth, feeding programs to malnourished children, micro-enterprise projects for widows and vulnerable families, and a variety of outreach programs.

Jennifer has ministered extensively throughout many different nations, seeing transformation come to some of the world's darkest and most broken communities. Through her ministry, thousands of children have been trained throughout Africa, Latin America, and North America. Her passion is to see a whole generation truly fall in love with Jesus and be released to partner with heaven. She longs to see the simple undiluted gospel restored in the church, and for the kingdom of heaven to manifest on behalf of the poor and marginalized.

Expression 58

For more information about
Expression 58 Ministries
please go to: www.expression58.org

GCM

To Donate or for more information
about Global Children's Movement
please go to: www.gcmovement.org

Jennifer has a variety of other teaching materials available including these powerful resources to help you activate your own children in the supernatural. For more resources please e-mail us at resources@expression58.org